PROTECTING THE PAST FROM NATURAL DISASTERS

CARL L. NELSON

THE PRESERVATION PRESS

NATIONAL TRUST FOR HISTORIC PRESERVATION

The Preservation Press
National Trust for Historic Preservation
1785 Massachusetts Avenue, N.W.
Washington, D.C. 20036

The National Trust for Historic Preservation is the only private, nonprofit national organization chartered by Congress to encourage public participation in the preservation of sites, buildings and objects significant in American history and culture. Support is provided by membership dues, endowment funds, contributions and grants from federal agencies, including the U.S. Department of the Interior, under provisions of the National Historic Preservation Act of 1966. The opinions expressed here do not necessarily reflect the views or policies of the Interior Department. For information on membership, write to the Membership Office at the address above.

Printed in the United States of America

95 94 93 92 91   5 4 3 2 1

Library of Congress Cataloging in Publication Data

Nelson, Carl L., 1948–
    Protecting the past from natural disasters / Carl L. Nelson
       p.   cm.
    Includes bibliographical references and index.
    ISBN 0-89133-178-6
    1. Structural stability.   2. Historic buildings — Conservation and restoration.   I. Title.
    TH845.N43   1991
    720'.28'8 — dc20   90-25730

Produced by Archetype Press, Inc.
Editor: Diane Maddex
Art Directors: Robert L. Wiser and Marc A. Meadows
Production Manager: Rebecca S. Neimark

Carl L. Nelson, formerly a staff member of the National Trust for Historic Preservation, is a writer in Washington, D.C., specializing in historic preservation and environmental issues.

♲ The text of this book was printed on recycled paper that meets the EPA mandate of containing at least 50 percent waste paper.

Cover: Fire in San Francisco's Marina district after the Loma Prieta earthquake, October 17, 1989. (AP/Wide World Photos)

Contents

Foreword

There is an unreported toll from natural disasters, one that may not be as immediately recognized as the tragic loss of life, limb or vital infrastructure. Yet this loss—of historic places—goes to the heart of America's towns and neighborhoods.

In the last third of this century, we have learned to reconcile progress with preservation. No longer do bulldozers strike with impunity, dismantling every historic building and neighborhood. To protect them, preservationists and public leaders have developed innovative strategies such as adaptive use and rehabilitation tax credits.

In the wake of the Loma Prieta earthquake and Hurricane Hugo, new lessons must be learned and applied. In many and various ways, preservationists must mobilize their forces and work with community leaders and government officials to plan how to preserve historic resources from natural disasters. In such emergencies residents and rescue workers often associate cleared rubble and rebuilding as a symbol of a community's resolve to continue.

Preservation can enrich our spirit of renewal by demonstrating that the landmarks of our past can be conserved, despite natural disasters. Sometimes as little as a second opinion by a structural engineer specially trained in historic structures can help save a building.

The historic preservation movement must reach out to the public and decision makers alike to educate them about new possibilities for preservation in light of unforeseen natural disasters. This book is an important first step, and I urge its reading and careful consideration by both planners and policy makers.

Pete Wilson
Governor of California

Foreword

A cyclone in 1713, a fire in 1838, the Civil War, an earthquake in 1886, tornadoes in 1938 — Charleston, a city that takes its history to heart, had seen its share of disasters even before Hurricane Hugo in 1989. They are part of our lore, and they have shaped our character.

Because historic preservation is integral to the lives of so many Charlestonians, it was no surprise that the individual and institutional responses of preservationists were central in our immediate and long-range recovery from Hugo. Charleston's preservation ethic meant that restoration, not demolition, was the order of the day. For those who considered demolition, the city's rigorous permitting process helped persuade them to restore instead.

Right after the hurricane, I sought an alliance of preservation groups to help guide us. The city's planning department staff and preservation officer, Charles Chase, responded quickly in rallying and coordinating Charleston's resources. The Historic Charleston Foundation, Preservation Society of Charleston, Charleston Museum and the Southern Regional Office of the National Trust, which is located in our city, were among the leaders as we sorted through debris and planned recovery strategies.

Throughout the recovery efforts Charleston was fortunate to have in place invaluable building-by-building historic resource surveys. And Hugo underscored for us something that we always understood — the value of maintaining our historic buildings. Old buildings that were in good condition before the hurricane came through much better than those that were run-down.

We who experienced Hugo hope that through this book others will be better prepared to protect and restore their historic properties when disaster strikes.

Joseph P. Riley, Jr.
Mayor of Charleston, S.C.

Preface

This book challenges Americans, particularly preservationists and public officials, to begin now to protect our heritage before the next — inevitable — natural disaster strikes. The two calamities of 1989, Hurricane Hugo and the Loma Prieta earthquake, offered an indisputable lesson: how well we prepare our historic places for the next emergency can and will make a difference in how well, or if, they survive.

By preparing for the certainty of the next potentially disastrous natural event — whether hurricane, earthquake, tornado, flood or fire — we may be able to save irreplaceable sites, objects and even whole communities from the consequences that flashed so vividly onto our television screens and newspaper pages. The first step in emergency preparedness has always focused rightly on protecting life. But we must ask what additional steps can be taken to protect our cultural and historic landmarks, the features and characteristics that make America's communities special places in which to live, grow and prosper. It is likely that those steps will in the process also promote public safety, by making much more secure the buildings in and around which we spend so much of our time.

The human costs of natural disasters are tremendous. Disorientation and severe emotional stress impair even the most calm and rational of decision makers, often leading to hasty actions that may do further harm to historic places. Planning in advance, for different types of natural events and threats, offers the only sure way of keeping to a minimum the destructive effects of disasters. Without planning, effective solutions for protecting the past from natural disasters will not be developed.

And without strong leadership — especially strong local leadership — such planning will not be undertaken before a disaster and cannot be implemented during one. Of course, federal and state government officials have important roles to play, as do private preservation organizations, managers of individual historic sites, owners of historic houses and our allied professionals. But experience proves that the key leadership role in preparing for natural disasters and coordinating responses to them is best exercised by local governments.

This book outlines the process by which all players can prepare for and weather disasters. Given the mission of the National Trust, our goal was not to publish an overall primer on disaster preparedness. Instead, our focus here is on historic buildings themselves, rather than general matters of safety or objects and collections; other publications and organizations are already addressing those issues. This book also is nontechnical in nature, because we want to stress planning and mitigation measures that public leaders and preservationists can carry out; other publications and groups similarly address the very technical aspects of this subject, many of which are cited here. And we have focused on major calamities such as hurricanes and earthquakes, both because of the immediacy of the 1989 disasters, and the lessons they taught for preservation, and because it is wise to prepare for the worst.

Protecting the Past from Natural Disasters is a clear call to action. It is the product of much thought by preservationists and disaster preparedness professionals, and it was made possible in part by members of the National Trust and agencies such as the National Endowment for the Arts that gave generously after the recent disasters—so that we all can be ready the next time around. I hope that this book encourages public planners, preservationists and owners of historic properties to join together as partners in the worthy cause of keeping America's heritage alive for many future generations. The United Nations has designated the 1990s as the International Decade for Natural Disaster Reduction, and we as preservationists must begin to do our part.

J. Jackson Walter, President
National Trust for Historic Preservation

Acknowledgments

A large number of people made substantial contributions to publication of *Protecting the Past from Natural Disasters:*

Diane Maddex, president of Archetype Press, developed the book and directed all facets of its preparation, editing and production. Her colleague Robert L. Wiser designed the book, with production assistance provided by Marc Alain Meadows and Rebecca S. Neimark.

The work of two persons in particular proved especially valuable because of the thought and research that each has devoted to protecting historic places from disasters: John E. Hunter, supervisory staff curator in the National Park Service's Curatorial Services Division and one of the agency's key experts on emergency preparedness; and Barclay G. Jones, AIA, AICP, professor in the Department of City and Regional Planning, Cornell University. Both have published significant materials on this subject, noted throughout the book and in Further Reading, and gave generously of their expertise.

National Trust staff members contributed helpful information and contacts and reviewed the manuscript, among them Peter H. Brink, vice president for programs, services and information; Elizabeth F. "Penny" Jones, director of preservation services; Susan A. Kidd, director of the Southern Regional Office; Kathryn A. Burns, director of the Western Regional Office; Courtney A. Damkroger, field representative, Western Regional Office; George Siekkinen and H. Christopher Slusher, both architects in the Department of Stewardship of Historic Properties; and Buckley C. Jeppson, director of The Preservation Press.

Damage assessment reports compiled by several professionals for the National Trust following the disasters of 1989 were particularly useful in preparing this book: for the Carolinas, William Chapman of the University of Georgia; Puerto Rico, C. Richard Bierce, AIA, Alexandria, Va.; Virgin Islands, Frederik C. Gjessing and George F. Tyson, St. Thomas, V.I.; and California, Bruce D. Judd, AIA, Architectural Resources Group, San Francisco. Another important report on California with policy recommendations was prepared by John F. Merritt, executive director of the California Preservation Foundation, with support from the Trust's Critical Issues Fund.

Others who provided helpful information and advice are Polly Arenberg, National Institute for the Conservation of Cultural Property; Martha Catlin, Advisory Council on Historic Preservation; Charles Edwin Chase, preservation officer-architect, Charleston, S.C.; Christopher Clark, American Institute of Architects; Jan Coggeshall, former mayor of Galveston, Tex.; Linda Dishman, National Trust advisor, San Francisco; George F. Farr, Jr., director, Office of Preservation, National Endowment for the Humanities; Carol Gould, education coordinator, National Preservation Institute; Ed Heidig, Office of Governor Wilson; H. Ward Jandl, chief, Technical Preservation Services, National Park Service; D. Anne Lewis, ASLA, director of business development, Loomis, Debenport, Boulton; Vincent Marsh, secretary, Landmarks Preservation Advisory Board, San Francisco; John Meffert, executive director, Preservation Society of Charleston; Lauren Meier, landscape architect, Preservation Assistance Division, National Park Service; Carney Moran, engineer, Federal Emergency Management Agency; Jonathan H. Poston, director of preservation programs, Historic Charleston Foundation; Sarah Rosenberg, director, American Institute for Conservation of Historic and Artistic Works; and Marcia A. Smith, Advisory Council on Historic Preservation. The initial development of the book was assisted by Timothy B. McDonald, Tacoma, Wash.

Appreciation goes to the many persons who contributed the special statements used throughout this book, including Gov. Pete Wilson of California; Mayor Joseph P. Riley, Jr., of Charleston; and National Trust President J. Jackson Walter. Others are Annalee Allen, president, Oakland (Calif.) Heritage Alliance; Adele Chatfield-Taylor, president, American Academy in Rome, New York City; Conrad D. Festa, senior vice president for academic affairs, College of Charleston; Melvyn Green, Melvyn Green and Associates, Manhattan Beach, Calif.; Eric Hertfelder, executive director, National Conference of State Historic Preservation Officers; Preston Hipp, director, Charleston Habitat for Humanity; Jerry L. Rogers, associate director for cultural resources, National Park Service; Kathleen Stratton, Legal Aid Society of Santa Cruz County (Calif.); Wallace E. Stickney, director, Federal Emergency Management Agency; and Lawrence Walker, executive director, Historic Charleston Foundation.

The National Trust also is grateful to Mystic Seaport, the Galveston Historical Foundation and the J. Paul Getty Museum for permission to reprint portions of their emergency manuals here. Thanks also are due the National Endowment for the Arts and the members of the National Trust for Historic Preservation, without whose financial support this book would not have been published.

Special thanks go to Judy, who makes it all possible.

Carl L. Nelson

THE DESTRUCTION OF 1989 IN PHOTOGRAPHS

The National Trust's Drayton Hall outside Charleston was relatively unscathed by Hurricane Hugo — but two-thirds of its historic trees were uprooted or topped off. "It looks like we had a heavy artillery shelling here," said Assistant Director George Neil. (Jack E. Boucher, HABS)

Hurricane Hugo struck the Virgin Islands
with special force on St. Croix.
Thick masonry walls of occupied cottages
at LaVallée Plantation generally withstood
the winds, but roofs did not fare as well.
(George F. Tyson)

On the north side of St. Croix, the early
18th-century town of Christiansted
suffered damage to three-quarters of
its historic buildings. Among its losses
was the Wesleyan Holiness Church.
The impact of high winds was
especially evident in higher elevations.
(Frederik C. Gjessing)

Most of St. Croix's 300 historic plantations
showed visible effects of Hurricane Hugo.
The abandoned great house at Estate Richmond,
a National Register property,
lost its second and much of its first story
as a result of the hurricane's winds.
(George F. Tyson)

THE DESTRUCTION OF 1989

This theater in Naguabo, Puerto Rico,
lost its sign and marquee among other damages.
It was one of many undocumented but potentially
historic structures affected by the hurricane.
Naguabo, on the southeast coast,
was hit hard because winds were channeled
through a narrow river valley into town.
(C. Richard Bierce)

Street furniture and monuments
in Puerto Rico were not spared by the storm.
This statue in San Juan
was decapitated by falling tree branches.
(C. Richard Bierce)

When the eye of Hurricane Hugo
passed over Charleston, S.C., it coincided
with high tides to produce violent storm surges.
Roofs were often the first to go,
and many historic buildings were flooded.
By the time the hurricane departed,
the Irish Volunteer Armory
was only a shell of its pre-Hugo self.
(Jack E. Boucher, HABS)

Buildings that were not well maintained,
such as this former warehouse on Hayne Street,
were easy targets of the hurricane.
(Jack E. Boucher, HABS)

Falling trees in the storm's path
brought damage to historic places everywhere.
At Boone Hall Plantation near Charleston,
roofs of the slave cabins
could not withstand the downed branches.
(Jack E. Boucher, HABS)

Historic interiors such as
the Second Presbyterian Church in Charleston
suffered particularly from moisture
that damaged decorative plasterwork.
(Jack E. Boucher, HABS)

THE DESTRUCTION OF 1989

Repairing the city's roofs was one of
Charleston's major post-Hugo tasks.
This building on upper King Street was already
in poor condition before the hurricane.
It did not survive after its roof gave way.
(Jack E. Boucher, HABS)

Charleston's 20th-century landmarks
were not spared in the hurricane.
The Art Deco–style Riviera Theater
was one of the King Street buildings affected.
(Jack E. Boucher, HABS)

THE DESTRUCTION OF 1989

Nearly all of the more than 300 historic
properties on Sullivan's Island, S.C.,
bore some aftereffects of Hurricane Hugo.
This frame house was one of a number
flattened by the powerful storm.
The 1.75-square-mile island, which faces south
toward the Atlantic Ocean near Charleston,
has had to withstand
frequent hurricanes and tropical storms.
(William Chapman)

Charlestonians used plastic sheeting
for quick weatherization to prevent additional
water damage. This Broad Street house
lost part of a wall, a chimney and a tree.
(Jack E. Boucher, HABS)

St. Luke's A.M.E. Church, located on
Highway 17 north of Charleston,
was a landmark for the local black community.
The 1908 building, abandoned before the storm
for a modern church, was uncataloged

This large tree fell into the Pfaff House
in Salisbury, N.C., a typical sight
in Hugo's wake throughout North Carolina.
(William Chapman)

Across the country, the Loma Prieta earthquake
left its imprint on historic buildings
and towns in California. Oakland's Art Deco
landmark, the Paramount Theater,
survived the tremor but with noticeable cracks
in its decorative plaster walls.
(Dexter Dong, *Oakland Tribune*)

Government in Oakland was disrupted
when its Beaux Arts city hall
sustained interior and exterior cracking.
Scaffolding like this became a prevalent
postquake sight around town.
(Pat Greenhouse, *Oakland Tribune*)

THE DESTRUCTION OF 1989

Loma Prieta shook out major sections
of San Francisco's Golden Gate Bank building.
The Historic American Buildings Survey
used photogrammetry to record the damage

This Queen Anne–style bungalow in Watsonville
showed obvious structural aftereffects
of the Loma Prieta earthquake.
(George Siekkinen, National Trust)

The Hotel Oakland was one of many
residential hotels damaged in the quake,
causing serious housing problems.
One of the rooms was Morgan Chin's.
(Reginald Pearman, *Oakland Tribune*)

LESSONS FROM HUGO AND LOMA PRIETA

For preservationists, a major aftershock
of the Loma Prieta earthquake was demolition
of buildings that might have been restored.
The Cooper House in downtown Santa Cruz
was razed despite pleas to save it.
(Judith Calson, *San Francisco Examiner*)

THE TWO DISASTERS that occurred

in fall 1989 — Hurricane Hugo and the Loma Prieta earthquake — brought devastation to the Caribbean and the East and West coasts within just one month, wreaking havoc on small towns and big cities alike. These natural calamities are powerful reminders that hurricanes, earthquakes, tornadoes, floods and catastrophic fires can occur practically anywhere in the United States. Their strongest lesson for preservationists is that it is possible to protect many, if not most, of our historic places from disasters. How to adequately prepare for, respond to and recover from the next natural disasters are the subjects of this book — because the question is not if, but when and where, disaster will strike next.

Wins and Losses

How did historic places do in the hurricane and earthquake? The short answer is that structures in good condition fared well, overall, during Hugo and Loma Prieta. Some buildings were damaged enough to warrant demolition; most were not, however. A number of historic structures in California that probably could, and should, have been saved were demolished. Landscapes, one of the most vulnerable historic resources in a storm, proved hard to protect, especially from the hurricane.

Hugo's tremendous winds taxed the stamina of historic buildings, sucking off roofs and punching out windows, thus leaving historic interiors open to water damage from flooding and a severe soaking from several inches of rain during the next few days. The storm also churned up acre after acre of historic gardens, natural landscapes and forests.

Following the California earthquake, it became clear that old buildings constructed before adoption of stringent seismic codes suffered the most, particularly unreinforced masonry, wood and stucco buildings built on soft, unstable soil, such as in San Francisco's Marina district.

"It goes without saying that saving human lives and rushing relief to the suffering or displaced is top priority in such times," National Trust President J. Jackson Walter told a National Public Radio audience a few months later. "Then people pick themselves up, dust themselves off and look around, and search out the old, familiar and long-loved landmarks."

What happened to the historic downtown of Santa Cruz, Calif., near the epicenter of the quake, is a case in point. Called the Pacific Garden Mall, the area underwent economic revitalization in the 20 years before the Loma Prieta earthquake and was added to the National Register of Historic Places. Rehabilitation from paint to new awnings helped revive what had been a dying historic district. There was an Achilles' heel to Santa Cruz's revival, however: seismic retrofits, which can be expensive and must be done sensitively in historic buildings, were only encouraged, not required.

Santa Cruz writer and artist Tom Killion described the results in the *Los Angeles Times* a month after the quake. "Pacific Avenue remains cordoned off behind a cyclone fence as cranes and bulldozers destroy, one after another, the Victorian-era brick and wood buildings that gave this town its charm," Killion wrote. "The mayor of Santa Cruz, Mardi Wormhoudt, has reminded us that 'the heart of Santa Cruz is its people, not its buildings,' yet we feel a deep sense of loss when we stand outside the fence that separates us from what was once the social and economic center of our community. . . ."

The Cooper House (1894) in Santa Cruz was one of the major buildings lost. A Romanesque-style former courthouse that survived the 1906 earthquake, it had been downtown's centerpiece since the 1970s, when it was adapted for shops and restaurants. Only 10 days after the building was damaged by Loma Prieta, the wrecking ball first crashed against its facade, bringing out hundreds to watch in sadness, a man with a saxophone to play "Auld Lang Syne" and, finally, newspaper headlines that read: "Soul of Santa Cruz Demolished."

Said Killion: "I paused in front of the empty space where the Cooper House had stood and looked across the rubble toward a stucco shopping mall untouched by the quake. Would this be the image of the new Santa Cruz?"

The Toll of Devastation: Hurricane Hugo

For six terrifying days — from September 17 through September 23, 1989 — Hurricane Hugo viciously assaulted, one by one, the Virgin Islands, Puerto Rico, South Carolina and North Carolina. Left in the wake of the storm were vivid reminders in the form of damages to property of all kinds. Astonishingly, loss of life directly attributable to the storm was small. But the widespread suffering caused by the loss of homes, livelihoods, personal property and personal injury was great.

In this assault of near-record magnitude, Hugo left its destructive mark on the enormously rich and tremendously varied collection of historic, prehistoric, natural and cultural resources along its path, scars that will always be detectable to those with a discerning eye. One of the most devastating storms of the century, the hurricane damaged at least an estimated 7,000 irreplaceable resources and caused hundreds of millions of dollars in losses to historic places.

THE PATH OF DESTRUCTION

Hurricane Hugo traced a westward arc through the Caribbean, passing directly over the Virgin Islands and the eastern part of Puerto Rico. Then it continued on a more pronounced course to the northwest toward the South Carolina coast, where it moved inland and turned north toward North Carolina. The intense storm finally dissolved in torrential rains over West Virginia and the Ohio River valley.

Hugo began by entering the Caribbean on September 16, slamming into the island of Guadaloupe with 150-mile-per-hour winds. Weather forecasters projected a path to pass 50 miles to the south of St. Croix, V.I., at a rate of 15 miles per hour. But on the afternoon of September 17, the storm veered north on a course directly for St. Croix and gathered intensity and wind speed. Gale-force winds began to topple power lines by mid-afternoon, and the islands were soon cut off from the outside world.

The Virgin Islands. The main mass of the storm pummeled the islands for periods extending beyond 14 hours. St. Croix experienced sustained wind velocities in excess of 200 miles per hour. Many tornadoes caused a series of extraordinarily violent and seemingly random pockets of destruction throughout the island, amplifying the direct effects of the wind itself.

St. Croix suffered the greatest losses to both natural and built environments because the storm remained over the island for such an extended period. St. Thomas was partially protected by rugged terrain, and St. John was spared most of the severe losses experienced elsewhere. Sea surges in the wake of Hugo did extensive damage to the south shores of both St. Croix and St. Thomas, even though rain during the storm was relatively low in volume.

An example from the historic old town of Charlotte Amalie on St. Thomas clearly demonstrates the force of the storm. The Anglican Cathedral of All Saints at first inspection seemed only slightly damaged by the loss of shutters on the north and south sides of the building, plus a few leaks in the roof. A closer study, however, revealed that the hurricane had created enough movement in the north side of the roof to snap two of the heavy tie-rods that link the north and south walls, a key part of the heavy trusses that are the main support of the roof structure. The force of the storm also severed some of the bolts anchoring the trusses to the walls. In short, this historic cathedral nearly collapsed.

The National Trust's survey of damage in the Virgin Islands revealed that historic places had taken a crippling blow. Hurricane Hugo damaged approximately 50 percent of the territory's historic structures and sites. About 46 percent of urban and 65 percent of rural historic places suffered harm. The good news is that only two percent were destroyed outright. The bad news is that the estimated cost of repairs amounted to more than $53 million.

Puerto Rico. The bad news was just beginning. On the morning of September 18, Hurricane Hugo made landfall in Puerto Rico. As the storm had accelerated on its passage from the Virgin Islands, it tore through the island in a hurry. Parts of Puerto Rico sustained winds up to and beyond 200 miles per hour, which in turn spawned tornadoes with their typically random destructive patterns. The storm charted a particularly slow and grinding passage over the small outer islands of Culebra and Vieques, producing heavy losses there as well as in the El Junque National Forest.

The San Juan Historic District suffered measurable damage to about 50 percent, or 375, of its structures, although most was not considered serious and no building was destroyed. About 60 buildings outside the district were heavily damaged. San Juan's historic district also received considerable damage to many significant landscape features, including several dozen trees at the El Morro fortress that went down in a controversial poststorm "cleanup."

Even though the damage may have seemed less dramatic and devastating than in some areas, it is feared that subtle, less immediately discernible effects such as hidden water infiltration may prove eventually to be as destructive as more obvious impacts.

South Carolina. Unfettered by the dragging and weakening effects of Puerto Rico's land mass, Hurricane Hugo became free to gain strength for the final assault on South and North Carolina to the northwest, where it made landfall on the evening of September 21.

As the eye passed directly over Charleston, wind speeds ranged from 120 to 135 miles per hour, with extremes even higher. The landfall also coincided with exceptionally high tides, producing storm surges of 17 feet above mean low tide. The blow thus was doubled in low-lying neighborhoods such as Charleston's Battery, where water poured in both through newly opened roofs and, on lower stories, from flooded streets.

Roof losses were extensive. "Anything that lost its roof had major water damage, not so much during the hurricane as on the Monday after, when we got five inches of rain," said Jonathan Poston, director of programs for the Historic Charleston Foundation. An estimated 80 to 90 percent of the city's building stock was damaged by the hurricane, including 89 structures that collapsed; 50 houses that were lost were in the city's historic core.

Hugo's winds scoured the city's historic peninsula, tearing into scores of its famous landmarks. Much of the roof was ripped from the City Hall (1801), as well as from the Market Hall (1841). Roper Hospital (c. 1850) lost much of its twin Italianate-style towers, and the steeple of Emmanuel A.M.E. Church (c. 1880) was toppled. Winds destroyed 30 percent of the city's public trees and 40 percent of all landscape trees.

Leaving Charleston, the storm cut a wide swath almost due north, affecting more than 20 counties in the eastern half of South Carolina, including Berkeley, Sumter, Dorchester, Orangeburg, Clarendon, Georgetown and Williamsburg counties. Berkeley County, one of the hardest hit, found that virtually all of its most historic properties sustained some damage. Surges and heavy rains ravaged beachfront communities such as Sullivan's Island, just north of Charleston, and McClellanville, 17 miles north. Winds lifted many Sullivan's Island buildings from their foundations. At McClellanville, mud and water flooded ground floors and blew apart houses and foundations. At the end of the storm, 18,000 miles of South Carolina roads were damaged or impassible, mainly because of fallen debris.

North Carolina. When it continued into southern North Carolina in the area around Charlotte the evening of September 22, Hugo still boasted winds in the 100-mile-per-hour range and continued to spawn tornadoes that were especially harmful to forested regions and landscapes. While 29 counties were declared disaster areas, most of the damage occurred in the nine counties surrounding Charlotte. The region is one of the most preservation aware in the state and was fortunate in that its state survey was "strikingly thorough," according to William Chapman of the University of Georgia, who conducted the National Trust's follow-up assessment.

Overall, about 200 historic buildings were damaged, most classified as minor except for the roof on the courthouse in Monroe. In Charlotte the worst damage was to three turn-of-the-century streetcar suburbs listed in the National Register of Historic Places: Dilworth, Myers Park and Elizabeth. Designed by Frederick Law Olmsted's firm and other renowned landscape architects, the neighborhoods were stripped of much of their tree canopy. A number of landmarks, such as the John Dinkins House (c. 1800), a Federal-style plantation house near Charlotte, lost roofs and chimneys. Trees fell everywhere: hundreds in Charlotte and 800 in one of Monroe's historic districts alone.

All along Hugo's path the damage was likened in the National Trust's assessment to "reverse building specifications, in which the objective is to remove and destroy rather than to build and preserve." Common effects included the following:

1 Roofs were damaged or blown off, endangering basic structural parts and interiors suddenly opened to the elements.

2 Torrential rains, wind-driven water, surface flooding and storm surges in coastal areas inundated structures with water.

3 Wind — sustained, pulsing and differential pressure — battered walls, trees and everything else in its path.

4 Buildings were partially destroyed through the loss of essential structural elements.

5 Wind-driven projectiles and falling structural elements and trees caused widespread damage.

6 Appendages such as porches, balconies, chimneys, gutters, downspouts, awnings and exterior lighting fixtures were stripped away.

7 Decorative embellishments including railings, finials, balusters, grilles, screens and fretwork became highly vulnerable to wind and falling debris.

8 Windows and doors had high degrees of failure, even with storm shutters; shutters were lost, glass broken and entire sections of sash and doors were torn out.

9 Moisture, some of it not immediately detectable, penetrated plaster, flooring, and mechanical and electrical systems.

10 Libraries, archives, museum collections and furnishings were blown about or damaged by water.

11 Public and private gardens and entire forests were devastated and defoliated by wind and water.

12 Urban areas lost streetscape elements such as outdoor sculpture, lighting fixtures, street furniture, fencing and signage as well as specimen trees important to historic spaces, parks and vistas.

13 Rural areas suffered losses to landscapes and structures.

14 Historic cemeteries were disturbed, with headstones and memorials knocked down.

15 Beaches were eroded, and archeological sites and abandoned ruins were scarred.

The following is a summary of estimated total losses to affected historic buildings, based on assessments generated locally during the three National Trust studies of hurricane damage:

	Damaged Structures	Repair Costs
Virgin Islands	1,258	$ 53,400,000
Puerto Rico	1,040	27,000,000
North and South Carolina	5,200	250,000,000
TOTAL	7,498	$330,400,000

AFTER THE STORM

The reaction to Hugo's profound destruction of historic places among preservationists and others was swift. Once the essential needs of the injured and those without shelter were met, organizations at the local, state and national levels began to send aid and volunteers to disrupted communities.

Virgin Islands. At the request of the state historic preservation officer, the National Trust's Mid-Atlantic Regional Office coordinated a joint team in St. Croix composed of staff from the Trust, American Institute of Architects, National Park Service and University of Georgia. The team of architects, preservationists and architectural historians examined damage to buildings listed in the National Register of Historic Places, reporting on more than 600 of them, and worked with members of the St. Thomas Historic Trust and other local preservationists. Technical assistance was also provided by the National Main Street Center of the National Trust.

Puerto Rico. AIA disaster response teams were on the spot in Puerto Rico immediately after Hugo passed through, helping assess damages and setting up a program to identify and mark historic structures. The state historic preservation office used a telephone survey of owners of National Register properties to obtain information about damages. Other participants in the recovery efforts included the Institute for Puerto Rican Culture, Puerto Rico Conservation Trust and Center for Advanced Study of Puerto Rico and the Caribbean. The city of San Juan, commonwealth government and National Park Service assessed the storm's effects on their own historic properties.

South Carolina. A "sea of volunteers," said the *Atlanta Constitution*, nearly overwhelmed Charleston within hours of Hugo—pouring in at the rate of 250 to 300 a day. The devastated town of McClellanville welcomed one volunteer for every resident.

In Charleston, the most affected of the state's cities, the mayor requested that the city's preservation officer, Charles Chase, lead the recovery charge. The following actions were soon launched:

1 An emergency stabilization and preservation task force, chaired by Chase and including the Historic Charleston Foundation, Preservation Society of Charleston, Charleston Museum and Southern Regional Office of the National Trust, met each morning at 7 a.m. to coordinate and evaluate recovery activities.

2 The Historic Charleston Foundation created a three-part preservation assistance program within 24 hours, including a database to keep track of outside contractors.

3 The Preservation Society of Charleston established the RESTORE program (Regional Emergency Support to Owner Rehabilitation Efforts) "to preach patience and perseverance" and promote proper rehabilitation.

4 Together, preservationists emphasized weatherization and stabilization over rushing to repair with inappropriate materials and techniques. They also helped negotiate funding for historically sound repairs with the Federal Emergency Management Agency.

5 Charleston's Board of Architectural Review greatly speeded up its review process, while maintaining its existing standards.

6 The National Trust helped initiate and fund the King Street Facade Design Assistance program for commercial buildings, which was managed by the city's downtown revitalization office with assistance from the Preservation Society of Charleston.

7 Several funds were established to aid owners of historic properties, including one created by the Historic Charleston Foundation, which it administered with the Preservation Society of Charleston and Charleston Museum; the foundation also managed another, the Architectural Monuments Fund.

Outside help came in numerous forms. A special team of National Park Service preservation experts went to Charleston to work with the emergency task force. Preservation students came from Mary Washington College, Clemson University, Roger Williams College, and the universities of South Carolina and Florida. The South Carolina Department of Archives and History, the state historic preservation office, set up a $100,000 emergency statewide grant fund for stabilization and repairs and surveyed damages throughout the state. State historic preservation offices in unaffected states such as Georgia and Virginia also sent in expert emergency teams, as did the Colonial Williamsburg Foundation to help with some of the major landscape restoration tasks. The Historic American Buildings Survey of the National

Hugo period for me was to see the tremendous equalizing effect the storm had on people. In addition to the obvious physical damage, the storm's winds blew down many of the social barriers that exist in cultures.

One story began when a young Amish boy from Pennsylvania came to Charleston for a specialized heart operation. Hurricane Hugo struck while the boy was still in the hospital. His parents were impressed by the care their child received in the midst of all the mayhem. In gratitude, the family went home and rallied a group of Amish men and women to come to Charleston to help rebuild houses for families in need.

First to be tackled was a new house for a family of six whose already dilapidated home was condemned after the hurricane. In less than a week these industrious visitors, carrying on an Amish tradition of pitching in after other disasters, had dried in a house. By the end of the week they helped another volunteer group finish another house. The spirit on the job site was miraculous. Cultural, economic and racial differences were laid aside for the common good and the need at hand. Today the first family helped is settled in its new three-bedroom frame home, a modern version of Charleston's famous single houses. The street it is on has been renamed — Hope Street.

Needless to say, Hurricane Hugo brought more suffering than it did joy, but it is a blessing to see what can be done when we unite to serve those around us in need.

Preston Hipp, Director
Charleston Habitat for Humanity

Park Service documented hurricane damages in photographs. The National Trust's National Main Street Center offered technical assistance to affected Main Street properties. And, because so many slate roofs were damaged in the hurricane, a local homeowner also took the initiative to form a company to import Welsh slate like that originally used on Charleston roofs.

North Carolina. With damage less severe than in South Carolina, recovery mobilization in North Carolina depended more on the state's own local and state governments. The state historic preservation office sent out site inspection teams, while many local planning directors and city preservation officers shouldered the burdens of advising owners of damaged historic properties.

National Trust. Early in October, the National Trust appealed to its members outside storm-impacted areas for donations to the Hurricane Hugo Crisis Fund for Historic Properties. They responded generously with contributions totaling $120,000 after expenses. In addition to direct disaster recovery aid, the monies raised by this mailing helped pay for the three studies cited in this book, with additional funding from the National Endowment for the Arts. The organizational response was targeted, first, to discover just what had happened to historic places in the affected areas; second, to assist with short-term stabilization; and third, to recommend strategies for longer-term restoration.

The Toll of Devastation: The Loma Prieta Earthquake

One month after Hurricane Hugo unleashed its wind and rain on the East Coast, at 5:04 p.m. on October 17, 1989, the Loma Prieta earthquake violently shook an area of California stretching from San Francisco and Oakland south to Salinas and Hollister. The epicenter occurred about 10 miles north of Santa Cruz and 60 miles southeast of San Francisco, and the quake ruptured a long semidormant 25-mile segment of the well-known San Andreas fault.

The magnitude 7.1 tremor lasted approximately 15 seconds and was the largest to hit the San Francisco area since the great quake of 1906. Its shocks were felt by nearly six million people in a region stretching from the Oregon border to Los Angeles. The number of people who lost their lives, fortunately, was small. But the region suffered 62 known deaths and more than 3,700 injuries. It also wreaked havoc on hundreds of historic buildings, particularly those constructed of unreinforced masonry. However, the percentage of historic buildings that emerged from the shocks unharmed was comparable to the total population of buildings that survived the earthquake, both historic and nonhistoric. The tremor caused an estimated $6 billion in destruction to property, in the process leaving 70 historic buildings beyond repair and another 472 damaged.

The Loma Prieta earthquake caused immense damage to northern California's historic buildings, preliminarily estimated at $350 million. Hardest-hit areas included San Francisco, Oakland, Salinas, and, in the epicenter of the quake, towns such as Santa Cruz, Los Gatos, Watsonville and Hollister. In addition to buildings that were damaged and subsequently torn down (see page 48), other damaged landmarks ranged from the Oakland City Hall and Santa Clara County Courthouse in San Jose to Mills Hall at Mills College in Oakland, the American Conservatory Theater in San Francisco and several buildings at Stanford University in Palo Alto (a victim also of the 1906 earthquake). Downtowns and Main Streets in Oakland, Santa Cruz, Hollister and Watsonville suffered such major losses that they will never look the same again.

But the shaking should not be blamed for much of the damage, because what happens during a quake—the physical process—as opposed to when it occurs, is entirely predictable, and hence may be prevented or mitigated. Even more so than in the case of Hurricane Hugo, buildings that were prepared for the possibility of earthquake—retrofitted and regularly maintained—were much more likely to survive with minimal damage.

The National Trust's damage assessment, funded in part by the National Endowment for the Arts, revealed that historic structures behaved as expected. The types of damage listed below appeared to be the most common result of the earthquake:

1 Cripple walls failed, causing otherwise intact wood-frame structures to slide or fall off their foundations. (A cripple wall is a short, wood-frame wall between the foundation and first floor of a structure that raises the first floor above grade level. Such walls are common in California residential construction of the late 19th and early 20th centuries.)

2 Unreinforced masonry walls cracked or collapsed.

3 Unreinforced masonry exterior walls of steel-frame structures collapsed.

4 Inadequately anchored exterior masonry facades collapsed.

5 Inadequately supported masonry parapets failed. Where walls or parapets supported an adjacent structure's roofs, these also tended to fail.

6 Masonry chimneys fell at the roof line.

7 Street-corner buildings, or those with inadequately supported ("soft") ground floors, collapsed or were severely damaged.

8 Interior plaster walls and ceilings cracked or collapsed.

LOMA PRIETA'S COSTS TO HISTORIC BUILDINGS

The following is a summary of estimated total damages to approximately 38,000 historic buildings, based on assessments generated by the National Trust study of earthquake damage:

	Damaged Structures	Demolished Structures	Repair Costs
Contra Costa County	1	0	$ 500,000
Alameda County	20	NA	500,000
Berkeley City	10	0	100,000
Oakland City	94	13	63,000,000
San Francisco City and County	92	7	44,800,000
San Mateo County	15+	0	30,000,000
Santa Clara County	100+	0	190,000,000
Los Gatos (town)	51	11	NA
San Jose City	24	2	3,500,000
Santa Cruz City	11	17	2,000,000
Watsonville City	23	5	12,600,000
Monterey County	10	0	NA
Monterey City	1	0	NA
Salinas City	NA	10	3,100,000
San Benito County	0	0	NA
Hollister City	10	6	NA
TOTAL	472	70	$350,100,000

NA: Not Available

ANOTHER AFTERSHOCK: DEMOLITION

One of the strongest sources of controversy in the immediate aftermath of the earthquake was the "red-tagging" of historic structures by building and other inspection officials—an assessment only that they were currently unsafe to enter but one that led to a number of demolitions. In some cases, community leaders believed that any action, including demolition, was better than no immediate step, thus indicating that they were in control of the situation. The problem became acute in cases where municipal officials and the general public interpreted red-tag designations and preliminary evaluations to mean "demolish immediately."

Playing tag with old buildings. Damaged, but possibly sound, historic buildings began to come down. The small town of Hollister quickly razed eight buildings, including a major historic landmark, the Odd Fellows Hall. Among the first to go, two days after the quake, was Salinas's Cominos Hotel (1874), a haunt of John Steinbeck that was mentioned in his novel *East of Eden;* preservationists had temporarily saved it from the wrecking ball earlier in the year. Santa Cruz lost half of its historic downtown buildings in the Pacific Garden Mall, a National Register historic district. Included was the previously mentioned Cooper House, which officials decided had to be torn down, even though the building stood separate from other buildings within the historic district, was cordoned off from public access and, ironically, was in the midst of a seismic retrofit. Downtown Watsonville took on the look of an old prize fighter's teeth. And San Francisco, Los Gatos, Oakland and other communities lost other landmarks.

One long, drawn-out case came to a close more than a year after the earthquake, when the St. George Hotel (1895), an anchor building in Santa Cruz's Pacific Garden Mall Historic District, was demolished after the city argued that it was a hazard and impeded the economic revitalization of the downtown. Preservationists determined that the landmark was, in fact, restorable, even following an intentionally set fire. A restraining order barring demolition was eventually lifted in fall 1990. With the razing of the St. George, the historic district had lost half of its historic buildings, leading the state preservation office to conclude that the district had finally lost its integrity and that it should be removed from the National Register.

City officials in Los Gatos took a much more patient approach to evaluating the structural worthiness of their historic buildings, and, as a consequence, a year after the earthquake its historic downtown seemed much further along toward regaining full economic health. For one, the city established a policy requiring the design of replacement structures to replicate the originals.

Providing alternatives to demolition. The National Trust's Western Regional Office and California Preservation Foundation quickly distributed information packages designed to provide alternatives to demolition. They were sent to city and county administrative offices, city councils, planners, preservation groups, architects and others. Included were lists of essential information such as qualified structural engineers, loan sources and suggested preservation strategies.

A month after the earthquake, the San Francisco Landmarks Preservation Advisory Board issued an advisory that pleaded for patience and perseverance. "As you know," the statement began, "the [earthquake] damage has created an emergency which required the Department of Public Works to cite many buildings as 'Unsafe' (Red Tag). Many of these structures contribute to San Francisco's architectural heritage and are repairable. A 'Red Tag' is not an order to demolish. It is not a condemnation. It is a statement that the structure is unsafe to enter right now, and that some kind of work (perhaps to a building next door) needs to be done before it can be occupied."

In the months after the earthquake, other organizations worked hard to protect historic buildings and to get the word out to the public and public officials that a red tag was not a ticket to demolition. Among them were the National Park Service, state historic preservation office, local chapters of the American Institute of Architects, California Office of Emergency Services, Foundation for San Francisco's Architectural Heritage, Oakland Heritage Alliance, Los Gatos Heritage, Pajaro Valley Historical Association, Palo Alto–Stanford Heritage, Hollister Downtown Association and Monterey County Historical Society. Teams from the National Park Service and state preservation office also offered expert advice in assessing damaged historic structures.

Using an allocation from the President's Discretionary Fund for Disaster Relief, the National Trust backed up the campaign with more than 30 emergency planning grants ranging from $500 to $5,000 and, in Washington, with a lobbying effort to secure emergency appropriations for earthquake relief. The Trust also committed funds from two of its financial-aid programs to demonstrate the viability of historic structures. The Critical Issues Fund, in cooperation with the California Department of Commerce, awarded a $25,000 grant to the California Preservation Foundation to support engineering and design assistance in the communities of Hollister, Santa Cruz, Watsonville, Salinas and Los Gatos. In addition, a practical handbook was written and two professional workshops were held, emphasizing appropriate methods for disaster preparedness. In the first month following the quake, the Trust also established a new Emergency Stabilization Loan Program in partnership with the Bank of the West. This program offered low-interest, short-term loans to stabilize historic structures, giving property owners immediate financial assistance and time to gain accurate information about the costs of rehabilitation. This loan fund later was expanded through partnerships with the Greater Santa Cruz County Community Foundation, United Way of Santa Cruz County and Pacific Western Bank.

The California legislature, in an emergency session only two weeks after the earthquake, enacted a strong law, Public Resources Code 5028, protecting national and local landmarks damaged by natural disasters, unless an imminent threat to the public exists. The law required approval by the state preservation office before demolition of any registered landmark in the aftermath of Loma Prieta and will continue in effect for future declared disasters.

Lessons from Hugo and Loma Prieta

In retrospect, the earthquake and hurricane both taught clear lessons for preservationists and government officials alike. These lessons can be summed up in two words: *maintain* and *plan*. The two disasters proved that historic places can be protected if they are in good condition, if emergencies are planned for, if steps are taken to mitigate forces that cannot be prevented, and if property owners, preservationists and public officials coordinate their efforts.

Specific recommendations for dealing with natural disasters — before, during and after — appear throughout this book and are summarized in the concluding chapter. The 1989 occurrences, however, provide the following immediate lessons:

1 Historic structures and landscapes that were well maintained were more likely to survive a disaster.

2 Most preservationists, public officials and property owners did not have formal disaster plans addressing the needs of historic places. Some museums, libraries and archival collections were better prepared.

3 The most effective leadership for disasters came primarily from the local areas affected — from government, preservation organizations and community leaders. Federal and state agencies may provide help, but the best leadership is local.

4 Many historic buildings require seismic retrofitting and other reinforcements to withstand strong earthquakes and wind pressure.

5 Surveys and inventories of historic resources in many localities are incomplete, making damage assessment and repair more difficult.

6 Declarations of a state of emergency may suspend (or be interpreted to suspend) environmental review and landmarks regulations or throw normal processes into disarray because damages lead to increased applications for review.

7 Building inspectors and engineers inexperienced with historic properties often are unfamiliar with the special attributes and requirements of historic properties and thus take action or make recommendations that are unnecessarily harmful or destructive.

8 Panic, emotional distress and a desire to return quickly to normal may result in pressures — by property owners, businesses, governments and the media — to demolish damaged structures that can, in fact, be repaired.

9 A rush to repair may result in substandard or incorrect work that further damages historic structures. In the rush, historic parts and features also may be thrown out with the debris.

10 Volunteers want to help. Some are qualified and self-directed; all need supervision and clear direction.

Despite the lack of formal emergency plans and networks, preservationists and public officials at all levels came together quickly — pitching in with exceptional cooperation to achieve immediate and long-term recovery.

WHAT DISASTERS DO TO HISTORIC PLACES

Some of the damage that disasters cause
is immediately obvious —
such as the wall of the Clay Building in Oakland,
which crumbled in the 1989 earthquake.
(Pat Greenhouse, *Oakland Tribune*)

NATURE is often the ultimate test

for historic places. "The mightiest works of the proudest humans are slight and fragile compared to natural forces," observed Cornell University Professor Barclay G. Jones in a 1990 issue of *Museum News*. "Currently, we depict nature as peaceful, benign and in need of our solicitous protection. By contrast, our ancestors viewed nature as terrifying elements to placate with homage and sacrifice and from which to seek protection from the gods."

Safeguarding historic buildings, interiors, collections and landscapes today begins with understanding nature — specifically, the risks posed by common natural disasters such as earthquakes, hurricanes, tornadoes, floods and fires. What happens during each of these occurrences and what effects they have on structures and settings is explained here.

When the Ground Moves: Earthquakes

One constant of the human experience is the expectation that the ground is solid and unmoving. But many thousand earthquakes occur throughout the world each year; in the United States perhaps several hundred of them are powerful enough to distract people from everyday life. The dramatic fall of part of one facade of the Hotel Oakland in Oakland, Calif., during the Loma Prieta earthquake demonstrated two things about the enormous power of these cataclysmic events: first, that a steel-frame building is well adapted to surviving the shaking stresses of a quake, and, second, if that same building is surrounded by unreinforced masonry curtain walls insufficiently attached to the frame, they may quickly be shaken into rubble. As long-time earthquake observers have noted, it is not quakes that kill people — it is buildings.

Steady creep. The crust of the earth, while certainly solid, on a large scale is composed of huge plates that are constantly moving in relation to each other. On the North American continent, the Pacific plate is plunging beneath the crust of the West Coast land mass, thrusting up the coastal mountain ranges. One of the main fracture lines where this dynamic action appears is called the San Andreas fault.

The San Andreas fault separates two land masses that are moving past each other, generally northward on the east and southward on the west, at an average historical rate of about two inches each year. Over decades, however, this steady creep can stop, allowing tremendous stresses to build up between the two opposing plates. Miles below the surface, when the strain has built sufficiently, something must give to bring things back into balance, at the same time releasing an incredibly powerful shock that can be felt, with sensitive instruments, worldwide. During the famous San Francisco earthquake of 1906, for example, the San Andreas fault reportedly moved 15 to 20 feet to restore the earth's equilibrium and, as a consequence, damaged many buildings and started fires that destroyed much of the city.

The Big One? It is the big earthquakes that command the immediate attention of all who feel them. Loma Prieta was one such seismic event, a 7.1 Richter scale temblor (the 1906 quake measured around 8.25 on the same scale, or 50 times the force). On the Richter scale, each whole-number increase in magnitude corresponds to a release of energy approximately 30 times as great. Powerful as it was, Loma Prieta was not the big earthquake that Californians have been waiting for.

The 1976 earthquake that struck the Chinese city of Tangshan claimed nearly a quarter million lives. In 1985, in Armenia, the death toll may have been 40,000 or more; in Mexico and Mexico City, 10,000 died. By contrast, the equally serious, or even stronger, Loma Prieta quake killed 62. The reason for America's good fortune: strong doses of luck and improved construction techniques, including retrofits.

But more earthquakes are just around the corner. A FEMA study concluded that only three states are free from quake risks — Florida, Mississippi and Texas. In addition to California, seriously in danger are Memphis, Tenn.; St. Louis, Mo.; Washington State; and parts of Utah, Idaho and Montana — as well as Charleston, S.C. The late director of the National Center for Earthquake Engineering Research, Robert L. Ketter, predicted that a catastrophic earthquake will strike east of the Rocky Mountains by the year 2000.

Loma Prieta, while not the disastrous quake predicted for California during the next 20 to 25 years, did set to rest one debate that had been raging for years. Has it been worth it to spend untold billions of dollars designing and retrofitting buildings to withstand seismic shock? The answer is a resounding yes, particularly for historic buildings.

What happens during earthquakes? The simple answer is vibrations. But these vibrations, like music, can be amplified in amazing, and catastrophic, ways:

1 Seemingly solid soil liquefies, particularly in landfill and flood-plain areas, leading to foundation failure and partial or complete collapse of buildings, as in the Marina district during the Loma Prieta earthquake.

2 Just as a tuning fork can shatter a glass, a building that cannot accommodate side-to-side shaking can resonate with the harmonics of the quake and collapse.

3 Some buildings, particularly old wood-frame structures, are not securely anchored to the ground. Earthquake vibrations may bounce these structures right off their foundations.

4 Similarly, in some buildings unreinforced masonry infill walls are not securely anchored to the structural framework. The wall, but not the structure, may collapse into rubble.

5 Larger structures with concrete frames and floor slabs may simply collapse in a "pancake" failure.

6 Damage increases with the strength and length of shaking. An earthquake's strength decreases rapidly with distance from the fault — it will be one-sixteenth as strong at 50 miles, for example. And the longer buildings shake (Loma Prieta was 15 seconds), the greater the damage.

Unreinforced masonry buildings. One of the biggest preservation problems in earthquake zones is unreinforced masonry buildings, often called UMBs or URMs. These brick, stone and adobe structures provide excellent support for their structures vertically, but when exposed to the side-to-side motions of earthquake forces, they may fail. The buildings may be steel-frame structures in which the unreinforced masonry forms a curtain wall, or they may be of lower bearing-wall construction. Thousands of them were built in California before the 1940s and are still in use. San Francisco alone has identified 2,100 UMBs, of which 770 are residential — with 20,000 dwelling units.

What are the weak links in UMBs during an earthquake? According to the Bay Area Regional Earthquake Preparedness Project:

1 Lack of steel or other reinforcements within the walls, so that they crack diagonally or buckle perpendicularly to the plane

2 Lime mortar that has lost its bonding strength

3 Insufficient anchorage connections, with walls not adequately tied to roof and floor elements

4 Insufficient shear connections between floors and walls, causing the walls to deflect and collapse

5 Poorly connected nonstructural elements, such as parapets, cornices and architectural decoration that can fall to the ground

6 Irregular configurations, particularly U, L or H shapes, which cause greater problems than square or rectangular structures

7 Weak diaphragms, such as wood-sheathed floors and roofs that cannot transfer high shear forces generated by heavy masonry walls

Because many UMBs are historic, retrofitting them poses preservation concerns given that it can seriously damage architectural integrity if not carried out sensitively. The cost of such retrofitting is another serious concern.

Wind and Rain in Tandem: Hurricanes

"The houses were indescribable; the gable was out of one, the chimney fallen from the next; here a roof was shattered, there half a piazza was gone, not a window remained. The streets looked as if piled with diamonds, the glass lay slivered so thick on the ground." This description of Charleston after a hurricane by Mrs. St. Julien Ravenel was not Hugo in 1989. In fact, it was in the 1860s, close to the end of the Civil War.

The word "hurricane" apparently is derived from the Spanish for the Carib Indian term "Juracan," meaning, simply enough, big wind. And the term "hurricane-force wind" derives from the early 19th-century Beaufort scale, invented by Sir Francis Beaufort, describing a wind that would allow no canvas to survive if raised on a sailing vessel. While these storms are called hurricanes in the Atlantic, they are known as typhoons in the Pacific and cyclones in the Indian Ocean.

Exactly how hurricanes form remains a subject of discussion among scientists. They usually start off the coast of Africa when water temperatures and prevailing weather conditions allow warm, moisture-laden air to rise tens of thousands of feet, in the process beginning to spin in a cyclonic, counterclockwise direction. This spinning mass of air and water, which eventually may develop a calm and clear "eye" in its center, moves west and, gaining strength as long as weather conditions allow, eventually collides with the land masses of North and South America and the Caribbean. When sustained winds exceed 74 miles per hour, a hurricane warning may be issued. The strongest wind speeds recorded over land in a recent U.S. storm occurred during Hurricane Camille in 1969, reaching 172 miles per hour. Buildings that are not locked down firmly in readiness for a hurricane — each part secured to the other and the whole to the ground — are prone to fail.

1 Roofs are particularly vulnerable to a hurricane's strong, seesawing winds. They can give way, allowing wind and water to surge through a building. Unsecured slates may peel off in the wind; metal roofs may roll up and off. Roofs with high gables may fly away. Roofs that hold tend to be well maintained and held down by fasteners compatible with the roofing and substrate.

2 Appendages not firmly anchored, such as porches, balconies, chimneys, gutters, downspouts, awnings and exterior lighting fixtures and wiring, are often stripped away entirely. Also at risk are decorative adornments including railings, finials, balusters, grilles, screens and fretwork.

3 Wind-driven objects and debris — trees, detached roofs, other parts of structures, unsecured street furniture such as trash receptacles, benches, tables, chairs, awnings, signs and light fixtures — become projectiles and smash into buildings and landscapes.

4 The combination of wind and rain pushes over entire walls and breaks structural members. It also rips out windows and doors, a common failure even with storm shutters (although they can be an effective preventive measure).

5 High water soaks and badly damages structures, sometimes rising 10 feet or more inside. When combined with a high tide, storm surge can be among a hurricane's most dangerous elements.

6 Once a roof, wall, door or window fails, moisture penetrates plaster, wood flooring, furnishings, and mechanical and electrical systems — some of this damage embedded within walls or otherwise not readily observable.

7 Landscapes, from trees, shrubs and flowers to garden structures to land forms themselves, are blown down, uprooted and flooded, sometimes with salt water. Heavy trees may damage other elements when they fall.

The Midwest's Number One Threat: Tornadoes

No storm is more violent than a tornado. And the broader Mississippi River valley of the United States holds the record as the most common locale for their occurrence. The why of it is simple. During prime tornado season in the spring, the cold fronts of winter continue to plunge southward out of the Canadian Northwest, only to meet up with balmy, moisture-laden air from the Gulf of Mexico. The results are predictable.

As the cold air, or cold front, shoots southward, it runs up on top of the warm semitropical air from the Gulf, sending it in turn spinning counterclockwise northward on the surface of the front. The common local effect is thunderstorms, which in themselves can do substantial damage to historic and nonhistoric buildings alike. But a tornado is another thing entirely. When this natural phenomenon of warm air seeking to rise becomes so localized and so intense, the circular winds themselves can surpass 300 miles per hour. The effects on all buildings are devastating.

One early account, a graphic depiction by George Milligen-Johnston in *A Short Description of the Province of South Carolina*, occurred in Charleston on May 4, 1761: "A terrible phenomenon resembling a large column of smoke and vapor. Its prodigious velocity gave it such a surprising momentum as to plow Ashley River to the bottom and to lay the channel bare. [The tornado tore] up trees, houses and everything that opposed it; great quantities of leaves, branches of trees, even large limbs, were seen furiously driven about, and agitated in the body of the column as it passed along."

COMMON TORNADO DAMAGES

1 A moderately severe tornado is quite capable of lifting the roof off a historic building and, in the process, sucking out and widely scattering the contents.

2 The most intense tornado can lift a frame building in its entirety, hurling it a considerable distance through the air.

3 Often, when a tornado passes over a structure, the rapid reduction in air pressure will cause the higher pressure inside to literally explode the building.

4 Most common, however, in buildings exposed to tornado winds will be the loss of roof elements, particularly those improperly maintained or inadequately connected to the roof substrate.

5 Tornadoes can be equally devastating to trees and historic landscapes, in many cases altering entire land forms beyond recognition.

Facing Troubled Waters: Floods

It will be a long time before Americans stop associating the city of Johnstown, Pa., with the word "flood." More than 100 years ago, on May 31, 1889, after three days of heavy rain, the citizens of this small town were worried about the rising waters of the Little Conemaugh River in the lower parts of town. But they were also worried, and rightly so, about the weak, inadequately maintained earthen South Fork Dam nine miles upstream. When the dam was breached by rising water, it wore quickly away, as quickly as if it were a sand castle wall exposed to a rising tide. Seventy-five feet of water was nearly instantaneously hurled downstream, directly at Johnstown, resulting in 2,200 deaths in a churning mass of rocks, debris and broken-up buildings. Yet another flood overtook Johnstown in 1972.

Flood plains. Of course, dam failure is only one cause of flooding, and it probably is the most easily preventable. The best thing to do is not build in the flood plain. But historic communities are often situated on a flood plain or near a navigable waterway. American history, in particular, is the history of communities built on the profits of waterborne commerce.

Many floods are predictable, using historical figures of rainfall and factoring in destruction of wetland and forest habitats by development upstream and potential obstructions caused by new bridges downstream. Seasonal flooding caused by spring thaws and rains is a typical example.

Storm surge. But there is another type of flood that, just as storm winds work to dismantle historic roofs, burrows in to undermine foundations and floods through doors and windows: storm surge, a combination of water pushed by the wind, high tides and low atmospheric pressure that allows seacoast water levels to rise to unthinkable heights.

On Saturday, September 8, 1900, one of the deadliest natural disasters ever to hit the United States unleashed a furious flood on Galveston, Tex. Dr. Isaac Cline, head observer for the National Weather Service in Galveston, experienced firsthand the awesome power of storm surge during this hurricane. (His posting of storm warnings against orders is credited with saving thousands of lives, although another 6,000 persons died.) Standing in his doorway at the height of the hurricane, nearly 10 feet above sea level, the water swirled around his ankles. In mere seconds, before he could move, the eddying waters were around his waist and, as the family retreated to the second floor, continued to rise for the next hour. Dr. Cline survived. His house, however, did not.

COMMON FLOOD DAMAGES

1 In contrast to other disasters, flood threats to historic structures often are entirely predictable and involve burst water pipes or heavy rains that inundate lower stories and basements, where off-display collections may be improperly stored.

2 Because historic buildings often are located in flood-prone areas, they are threatened not only by rising waters themselves, but also the flotsam of uprooted trees and other debris that floods can bring.

3 Sometimes floods outstrip the most pessimistic predictions. When the Arno River watershed above Florence, Italy, received 19 inches of rain during two days in September 1966, the resulting flood reached 20 feet in some squares of the ancient city. The river's waters, channeled by narrow streets, funneled at up to 80 miles per hour and poured into Italy's Nazionale Library, dowsing thousands of priceless manuscripts, exhibits and statuary.

Unnatural Disaster: Fires

"Fire," *Philadelphia Inquirer* architecture critic Thomas Hine once wrote, "is an extremely fast and effective means of deconstruction." And in most cases, fire is the disaster that humans visit on themselves.

Yet given the irreplaceable nature of historic structures and their collections, and the all-consuming nature of fire, it must be counted as a probability rather than a possibility. The most common failing in dealing with fire is the attitude exemplified by an anonymous museum director. When asked why he had not installed a modern sprinkler system in his museum, he told Stephen W. Musgrove of *Museum News*, "We're not planning to have a fire."

All fires, of course, start small. The smoldering short in the old coffee pot, the tangled spaghetti of wires behind the computer and the pile of paper plates left too near the not-turned-off stove can each begin a small conflagration that eventually engulfs a historic building.

During a disaster, the actual damages to historic structures are produced mostly by water and fire, regardless of the initial cause. But fire itself, in large part, is not a natural disaster (except for catastrophic ones such as forest fires ignited by lightning); rather, it is almost entirely preventable and caused by humans.

COMMON FIRE DAMAGES

1 Historic buildings often were built, at least in part, of combustible materials such as wood. As it has aged, this wood usually has dried, becoming even more vulnerable to fire. Intense fires may overwhelm heavy antique timber structural systems and cause the collapse of foot-thick exterior walls.

2 Historic structures generally are not compartmentalized. In a fire, the entire structure — rather than just a portion — is threatened.

3 Furnishings and collections, especially paper, also are excellent fuels for fire.

4 Even a small fire can cause serious smoke damage to historic structures and furnishings.

5 Water used by firefighters may compound a fire's destructive effects and in some cases do more harm than the flames.

6 Fires also have the ability to level historic forests and landscapes in their path.

BEFORE DISASTER STRIKES

Planning Measures

Keeping historic buildings in sound condition is a good — but not foolproof — way to prevent major damage in a disaster. This frame house in Puerto Rico lost its roof to Hurricane Hugo. (C. Richard Bierce)

DISASTERS HAPPEN—and because

they do, they loom as potentially enormous risks to historic places and their contents. Formulating a disaster preparedness plan and taking preventive measures will, in all probability, help mitigate the destructive effects when disaster strikes. Many of the losses inflicted on historic buildings and their contents can be avoided. Given the inevitability of natural disasters, a little prevention goes a long way in saving buildings, preserving our heritage, reducing money spent on repairs, and minimizing recovery time and its associated economic dislocations. There is no doubt that planning ahead can save both lives and historic places.

A number of preliminary questions can be asked as a prelude to becoming more prepared for any disaster:

1 What kinds of disasters are possible in a given location? What kinds are most likely?

2 Whose input is needed to develop a disaster preparedness plan?

3 How can the plan be communicated effectively to all participants?

4 Who sets policy? Who sets a plan in motion? Who is second in command?

5 How should resources—people and supplies—be organized?

6 What are the most important things to save?

America's heritage of buildings, landscapes, objects and documents is a public trust, held as much for generations yet to come as for the current occupants. It cannot be replaced. For everyone charged with protecting this heritage—from homeowners and preservationists who direct an organization or a historic site to public officials at all levels—disaster planning is a necessity. For each property and organization, it is likely to involve different assets, concerns and people. Yet for each the process can be carried out methodically.

Beginning the Disaster Planning Process

Disaster planning has two goals: (1) a contingency plan, designed to take effect when an unforeseen event strikes or is imminent, and (2) longer-term mitigating actions undertaken to minimize the impact of an anticipated event.

Where should preservationists and public officials begin the planning process? Fortunately, throughout the museum and historical communities with which preservation has such close ties, much thought has gone into disaster preparedness, and good models are available. John E. Hunter, the supervisory staff curator of the National Park Service's Curatorial Services Division, Harpers Ferry, W. Va., has written and provided extensive advice on disaster planning. Hunter, whose recommendations appear in the Park Service's *Museum Handbook* and are noted throughout this book, suggests the following as a systematic planning process especially suited for historic sites and museums; it can be adapted by private property owners, preservation managers and public officials to their own needs:

Assign responsibility for planning. A chief executive or director can be the disaster coordinator, but it is more effective for a staff person to be appointed to prepare the plan — both because of familiarity with everyday procedures and because staff will be responsible for implementing the plan.

Gather planning tools. Reference works should be collected, together with information from local and national disaster agencies as well as models of plans for similar organizations or cities.

Contact local protection agencies. Disaster coordinators should be in touch with police, fire and emergency agencies to let them know about potential needs in an emergency and also to determine the extent of those agencies' ability to respond when faced with a larger disaster.

Identify hazards and threats. Natural and other hazards should be systematically identified and analyzed to determine which ones may be threats and to assess the risks of damage. Priorities for dealing with them should also be set.

Identify and set priorities for historic resources. Together with inventories of individual sites, surveys of historic resources in a city or region should also be made. Priorities for saving these resources can then be established. Having a clear idea of priorities allows concentration on the most vital resources as a disaster develops and certainly afterward.

Formulate protection methods. Actions to prevent some losses, reduce others and generally prepare for a response during an emergency should next be developed and implemented. Part of this process involves setting priorities for recovery and determining what outside resources and supplies will be needed to cope with a disaster.

Plan for command and control. The disaster plan should change an institution or agency's priorities and methods, not its basic organization. Preparations should be made to go into an emergency operations mode using the existing structure and chain of command of the institution. The emphasis should be on flexibility, innovation and streamlined operations.

Write the plan. A written disaster plan is the next step, perhaps following the outline presented later in this chapter. Characteristics of a good plan, according to Philip Ward of the Canadian Conservation Institute, are that it be flexible, simple and adaptable; facilitate good communications; provide speedy responses; identify emergency priorities; single out all needed resources; and acknowledge sources of assistance.

Train staff in how to use the plan. Training guarantees that responsible employees will react automatically in an emergency, ensures that each person entrusted with responsibilities will know what to do, and provides the knowledge that each person needs to do the work without panic.

Test the plan. The first test should come when the written plan is still in draft. After the plan is adopted, periodic drills should indicate if it will function as intended. Whenever a test reveals deficiencies, the plan should be revised.

Evaluate the plan. If a disaster strikes, analyze how well the plan worked. Assess its components and the performance of all participants with written records and photographs. Obtain opinions from everyone involved through interviews and meetings.

Keep the plan current. The disaster plan should be reviewed regularly, every three to six months and never less than annually. Carefully record amendments by noting dates of changes, the nature of changes and pages affected. Maintain a list of plan holders to notify as changes are made. It is especially vital to keep names and telephone numbers up to date and to ensure that new staff are included in preparations. Review the plan with local emergency management officials, and make sure that they have a copy. Ask to be included in local emergency exercises.

Who Is in Charge? Making Policy Decisions

Who should set preservation preparedness policies? The answers are not simple, and they vary from community to community. Organizationally, preservation disaster planning should be done at the federal, state and local government levels; by each preservation organization and historic site, national, state, regional and local; and by all owners of historic buildings and collections. Because natural disasters have such immediate and harmful effects on historic places, only organizational responses can hope to ameliorate the damages. Each institution and property owner must formalize a disaster policy in a written plan and, equally important, must coordinate that plan with other organizations, governmental and private, that are themselves preparing to respond to a disaster.

As former National Trust Executive Director Robert R. Garvey, Jr., and Peter H. Smith write in *Protecting Historic Architecture and Museum Collections from Natural Disasters*, edited by Barclay Jones, "Those responsible for caring for cultural resources have a responsibility to develop firm policies to protect these resources in times of natural disaster. Much can be done to minimize damage to historic architecture and museum collections resulting from a disaster with planning and prudent actions. To do less is to fail in the responsibilities we have accepted and to treat our heritage with callous disregard."

PLANNING ALONE

Someone must be in charge during an emergency. Staff members and volunteers certainly can make suggestions, but the response to an emergency must be led — it is the job of the emergency plan coordinator, whoever that may be, to decide which jobs are necessary and when.

Private organizations. Disaster planning at a historic site or museum or within a preservation organization should begin at the highest level, with a committee of the board of directors or trustees. This group may provide suggestions to the staff who develop the preparedness plan and will have final say over the contents, the lines of responsibility and authority it contains, and the schedule for updating and implementing it. It also must fund the preparations.

The director of a historic site or organization will usually assume the responsibility of invoking an emergency plan. Disasters, on the other hand, do not always wait until the director is on site. And communications do not always work as advertised during an emergency. In fact, one of the key roles of onsite security staff during off hours may be to assume the temporary role of disaster coordinator.

Governments. For state, city and other local governments, emergency plan authorization rests with the chief elected officer — governor, mayor, city or county executive. This authority generally is delegated to a separate disaster planning agency or designated coordinator within another office.

Experience shows that in many cases, preservation has not been much or at all a part of the disaster planning process. Opportunities thus exist everywhere to introduce concerns for historic places into preparedness measures. Where there are official preservation offices or landmarks commissions, the avenues of potential cooperation are clear; in the absence of designated preservation agencies, it will be up to private organizations to fill the need, providing an advisory or coordinating role to ensure that preservation issues are not overlooked. Preservationists, for example, can seek to participate in municipal emergency groups and help draft disaster plans to ensure that preservation issues are addressed; such was the case in Los Gatos, Calif., where the planner who serves as staff to the landmarks board was a member of the team that developed the city's disaster plan.

For each given location, a different mix of policies will be necessary. Historic sites and cities in seismic zones and hurricane-prone areas will want to develop different policies toward possible disasters. In fact, the degree of predictability in many ways mandates disaster policy, because those historic places where the potential threats are known can adopt a systematic approach to undertaking preventive measures as well as preparing responses.

PLANNING TOGETHER

Given the nature of preservation — a multidisciplinary field cutting across private and public as well as local, state and national levels — coordinated responses to disasters are needed. While preservation comes down ultimately to the individual place to be protected, natural disasters are bound to affect more than just one site. What a city or a state must do to cope with a disaster is different from what a property owner or manager must do. The conclusion? Preservationists and public officials must work together to be ready for the next catastrophe.

Charts on the following pages outline some of the potential players and the roles they should begin to play on the national, state and local levels as well as at an individual historic or museum site:

1 The national preparedness network draws together federal agencies, national preservation organizations and professionals in allied fields to suggest policies, provide clearinghouse functions and furnish technical aid.

2 The state/territorial network is centered on working with the state disaster agency, the usual conduit for a state's emergency response.

3 The local network focuses activity where it is most needed in an emergency and can have the most immediate effect, calling for leadership by city or county government and local preservation organizations.

4 A historic site or museum's own preparedness group takes responsibility for protecting an individual historic property, working in coordination with local emergency services, preservationists and related professionals.

Any one of the groups indicated can take the lead in its own sphere or community to start the preparedness process before the next disaster.

National Preparedness Network

Federal Emergency Management Agency
Direct federal relief efforts, working with state governments

National Park Service
Provide expertise, statistics, documentation and, at times, technical assistance through Associate Director for Cultural Resources, Preservation Assistance Division, National Register of Historic Places, Park Historic Architecture Division, Curatorial Services Division and Historic American Buildings Survey/Historic American Engineering Record

National Trust for Historic Preservation
Serve as a clearinghouse for private disaster preparedness strategies and work with public agencies to improve disaster preparedness for historic resources; regional offices and museum properties participate at local levels

Advisory Council on Historic Preservation
Advise on preservation preparedness policies and review federal actions affecting properties listed in or eligible for the National Register

American Institute of Architects
Provide teams of architects for damage assessment and rehabilitation

National Conference of State Historic Preservation Officers
Coordinate disaster planning and responses by SHPOs

U.S. Geological Survey
Advise on disaster characteristics

U.S. Army Corps of Engineers
Provide construction expertise and assistance

U.S. General Services Administration
Advise on disaster planning and recovery for federal buildings

Preservation Action
Mobilize statewide coordinators for immediate and long-term legislative initiatives

Conservation and Related Professional Groups
Alliance for Historic Landscape Preservation
American Association for State and Local History
American Association of Museums
American Institute for Conservation of Historic and Artistic Works
American Society for Conservation Archeology
American Society of Civil Engineers
American Society of Landscape Architects
American Society of Professional Engineers
Association for Preservation Technology
Institute of Museum Services
Library of Congress
National Alliance of Preservation Commissions
National Endowment for the Arts
National Endowment for the Humanities
National Institute for the Conservation of Cultural Property
National Science Foundation
Smithsonian Institution
Society of Architectural Historians

State/Territorial Preparedness Network

Governor's Office
Establish state/territorial disaster preparedness agency and authorize disaster response

Disaster Preparedness Agency
Plan for and direct emergency response, providing liaison with federal and local activities

State Historic Preservation Office
Complete state historic resources survey, provide accessible data on affected historic sites, send technical assistance teams, ensure compliance with review procedures and process preservation funding as available

Statewide Preservation Organization
Where such organizations exist, coordinate private statewide assistance, using organizations and individual members' expertise

FEMA Regional Office
Provide official relief aid on behalf of FEMA and monitor funding that affects National Register properties

National Park Service Regional Office
Coordinate agency response, including assistance and documentation teams

National Trust Regional Offices and Advisors
Serve as liaison for National Trust and other private national preservation organizations. Provide direct technical and financial assistance for local preparedness and recovery efforts

American Institute of Architects Statewide Preservation Coordinator
Represent AIA in providing architectural planning and recovery aid

State Archivist/Librarian
Advise on protection and conservation needs of document and book collections

State Historical Society
Provide advice on historical collections and help in locating conservation experts

State Councils on the Arts and Humanities
Provide advice and funding as available, in coordination with the national endowments

Architecture Schools and Universities
Send teams of professors and qualified students to aid in recovery efforts

Preservation Action Coordinator
Suggest and support disaster-related preservation legislation

Local Preparedness Network

Office of the Mayor or City/County Executive
Establish local disaster preparedness office and authorize emergency response

Disaster Preparedness Office
Plan for and direct emergency response, working with public and private local preservationists to prepare for historic site needs

Local Preservation Agency
Coordinate planning and recovery for historic buildings and districts, including city-owned historic structures, and provide accessible inventory of historic resources

Landmarks Commission/Design Review Board
Develop emergency review procedures and assessment guidelines, complete local historic resource survey, process postdisaster applications for repair and new construction, and ensure overall compliance with design review processes

Nonprofit Preservation and Historical Organizations
Coordinate private preparedness and response, including providing planning and technical information for owners of historic properties and helping landmarks commissions develop review procedures

Historic Sites and Museums
Prepare for own sites and offer technical expertise as feasible after a disaster

AIA Chapter
Designate members qualified to guide or plan rehabilitation and restoration of historic buildings

National Trust Regional Office
Serve as liaison for National Trust

Other Local Representatives
Architect
Architectural School Dean
Archivist
Art Conservator
Bank Officer
Building Inspection Official
Building Trade Representative
Business Owner
Engineer
Fire Department Representative
Homeowner
Insurance Agent
Landscape Architect
Librarian
Media Publisher, Editor or Reporter
Neighborhood Association Leader
Photographer
Police Representative

Historic Site or Museum Preparedness Group

The following organization is based on the emergency plan of the J. Paul Getty Museum in Malibu, Calif. The emergency leaders and staffs indicated are drawn from permanent positions.

Emergency Plan Coordinator
Museum Director
Assistant Directors
Security Director
Assess the need for the emergency plan and declare it to be operational; direct all operations while in emergency status; continually reevaluate the state of the emergency, damage and responses and command staff based on these assessments; determine when to cease a state of emergency

Personnel Manager
Administrative Director
Personnel Director
Assistants
Deploy and redeploy personnel on museum property, including using essential personnel and establishing a safe area for nonessential personnel outside emergency areas. Report to the emergency plan coordinator

Media Manager
Public Information Officer
Education Director
Special Events Coordinator
Oversee all external communications during the emergency; gather, compile and coordinate information for dissemination through the media, working closely with the museum director and other officials; act as liaison with outside agencies and the community as directed by the emergency plan coordinator; serve as liaison to families of employees and visitors; manage all outside telephone communications. Report to the emergency plan coordinator

Collections Manager
Curators
Registrar
Assistants
Direct emergency operations involving collections; oversee salvage, preservation and restoration activities; supervise technical areas including conservation assessment and treatment, packing, transportation, storage and documentation of treatment. Report to the emergency plan coordinator

Protective Services Manager
Security Director
Assistant Directors
Facilities Manager
Grounds Superintendent
Building Engineers
Coordinate all logistical support for emergency operations; take responsibility for the safety and welfare of all persons on the premises; oversee site security; allocate and distribute equipment and supplies; maintain the physical integrity of the buildings. Report to the emergency plan coordinator

Assessing Hazards and Vulnerability

To know what to plan for, an important first step is to have a good idea of what dangers threaten historic buildings and places.

ASSESSING DANGER

Barclay Jones of Cornell University has identified three separate components in assessing danger to historic places:

1 Hazard: the probability that a disastrous event of a certain size and severity will occur in a particular place.

2 Vulnerability: the amount of loss from a disaster of a certain size and severity.

3 Risk: probable loss from natural disasters of different kinds, considering the hazard probability against the vulnerability of the historic resources.

Assessing potential disaster risks requires an analysis of the hazards and vulnerability, determination of acceptable levels of risk and development of reasonable preventive measures.

Analyzing Hazards. That emergencies of varying kinds will occur is certain. The goal of hazard assessment is to find out what kinds of dangers are possible and how likely they are to happen. In planning for disasters of nature, it is wise to be prepared also for the full range of emergencies that can occur, from the disasters detailed here — earthquakes, hurricanes, tornadoes, floods and fires — to thunderstorms, blizzards, even volcanic eruptions and, outside the realm of natural disasters, emergencies such as industrial accidents, utility breakdowns, bombings, burglaries, vandalism, civil disorders and war.

Analyzing hazards, especially for natural disasters, should take two primary forms. By examining the historical record it is possible to gain useful knowledge of disaster threats to the region as a whole. Personal interviews, Weather Service records and newspaper archives all can contribute to making this broad assessment. For a particular historic place, a detailed technical examination of the site, structures, contents and landscapes is necessary. This exploration will reveal hazards at the micro level and allow them to be categorized into the broader groupings that actually cause damages: movement of the earth, water action and wind.

Once potential hazards are identified, attention can be turned to the historic place or sites to be protected.

Assessing Vulnerability. Barclay Jones notes that damages to historic structures can be grouped in three broad categories: kinetic effects, chemical effects and bacteriological effects.

The *kinetic effects* include those caused by vigorous motion, and the consequent damages are physical deformation. This means not only the window struck by slate roofing tiles hurled in a hurricane and the proverbial straw driven two inches into a tree trunk in a tornado. It also encompasses brick spalled by the tremendous pressure exerted when water freezes and thaws.

The *chemical effects* reveal changes in composition of the object or structure. The action of fire is perhaps the most dramatic one. But these effects also include the equally damaging immersion in water or long-term exposure to atmospheric pollutants. One of the most common is rust.

Immersion in water is usually followed quickly by the third class of damages: *bacteriological effects*. Mildew, mold and fungus can begin rapidly to break down historic structures and objects. This category might more accurately be named biological, as the action of insects and rapid weed growth also can overwhelm the structural integrity of a historic place.

Determination of risk. Actual risk is hard to pinpoint with scientific certainty because so many variables exist. As John Hunter of the National Park Service advises, "An uncomplicated approach to determining risk is to employ the concept that the more ways that a particular event (such as water damage) can occur under given circumstances, the greater the probability that it will occur and, thus, the greater the risk." He urges that disaster planners follow the following guidance: be ready for anything, no matter how small the risk.

Finding Historic Resources at Risk

The importance of preparing surveys of historic resources in advance of the next disaster cannot be overemphasized. They are a crucial part of the disaster planning process. Whether for a state, city, neighborhood or individual historic property, surveys tell preservationists and public officials what is worth saving — where the historic districts are, which structures are designated landmarks, whether any significant site is about to be demolished. After a disaster, surveys allow priorities for rescue work to be set and repairs to be carried out efficiently. They also provide a road map for assessing damages and planning recovery.

Both Hurricane Hugo and the Loma Prieta earthquake were surprises to preservationists, who then found out how difficult it was to provide answers about damages to historic places. When community leaders and legislators received preservationists' appeals for emergency help, they asked some predictable and fair questions: How many historic buildings and sites were damaged? How much will restoration cost?

Admittedly, even with accurate and comprehensive surveys, these are hard questions to answer, and they give rise to others: How can storm damages be assessed, particularly to one-of-a-kind historic structures and objects? Will hidden damages show up in a year or two or three? What about the effects on tourism, losses that may show up only when anticipated tax revenue short-falls appear a year later?

These are all difficult questions to answer, but the "biggest problem was simply that the numbers were not there," says William Chapman of the University of Georgia. At the request of the National Trust, after Hurricane Hugo Chapman conducted an analysis of state surveys of historic places in the South.

SURVEYS: PRESERVATION'S BOTTOM LINE

The National Historic Preservation Act of 1966, which created the national historic preservation program of today, launched the establishment of state historic preservation offices. As the first of their responsibilities, Congress required the SHPOs, in cooperation with federal and state agencies, local governments, and private organizations and individuals, to "direct and conduct a comprehensive statewide survey of historic properties and maintain inventories of such properties."

But the task of carrying out surveys has proven to be harder than it may appear. In spite of efforts over the past quarter century, combined in cases like Charleston with survey work by local organizations going back to the 1930s, the results of many surveys were not usable after the latest disasters hit. As Chapman reports, "It is as if we had been rehearsing for a play—and then flubbed our lines."

So what went wrong? Chapman notes that surveys "are 'multifunctional' in their orientation." Many survey results that appear completely logical and useful to preservationists may seem somewhat incomprehensible to public officials and legislators pressed with finding real solutions to serious problems during an emergency. Some surveys have looked at districts as a whole, without listing individual buildings on separate forms, as in the case of the Charlotte Amalie Historic District in the Virgin Islands.

Even in the face of enlarged responsibilities and declining budgets, states are experimenting with making their survey efforts more comprehensive and useful. Chapman's study found that survey work has evolved with the broadening interests of the historic preservation movement as a whole. While some states, Chapman reports, have done what might be called selective surveys of clearly eligible National Register sites, in large part states have echoed the growing interest in vernacular architecture and historic buildings in their contexts. This approach results in big numbers. Stephens County, Ga., in one of these more comprehensive surveys, exceeded state estimates for pre-1941 properties by 250 percent.

It is difficult to adequately evaluate the reams of information that results from such a survey. But to be useful during a disaster, surveys, regardless of their multiple purposes, must be able to rapidly produce real statistics and other data helpful in recovery efforts. They also must be up-to-date and include a photograph or physical description that provides a comparison point for evaluating any damage.

RETHINKING THE SURVEY FOR DISASTERS

What should be done? Rethink the survey effort altogether, Chapman advises. What good is a survey containing long written descriptions of a property if it sits not tabulated in a file drawer? Because, after Hurricane Hugo, that is where most of the survey material on historic structures was: gathering dust in file drawers. Neither time nor funds had been allocated to make the information accessible or "manipulatable," i.e., entered into a computerized database that would allow rapid calculation of damage estimates and restoration costs. The experience from both coasts was that computerization of survey information can be a boon in an emergency. Even systematizing building department and landmarks data can help, as San Francisco preservationists found out; it was difficult to compare lists of red-tagged buildings with the landmarks list, because the landmarks information had been compiled on a different, lot-parcel basis.

A National Conference of State Historic Preservation Officers task force on surveys recently suggested components of a model survey form:

1 Identification of the property, with location information

2 A short description or photograph

3 Statistical data, such as basic information on use, construction materials and approximate date of construction

4 Name of the surveyor

The NCSHPO further recommended that surveys attempt to identify all pre-1940 structures using short forms that can be completed in the field, with tabulation and evaluation taking place at a central office, probably using entirely different staff.

"The experience of the 1989 disasters," said Jerry L. Rogers, associate director of the National Park Service, "showed that inventories of historic resources—a key component of state and local government preservation work—were not fully effective planning tools. They were in many cases inadequate to assist decision makers in responding rapidly in these emergency situations. SHPOs and the National Park Service thus have begun working together to improve the ability of statewide surveys to be a part of the recovery process in the future."

Developing a Preparedness Plan

Prevention is a good motto when planning for disasters. In large measure, preparedness plans consist of common sense leavened with long lists of things to do, responsible parties and telephone numbers. While simple in concept, developing a good one requires considerable thought and, equally important, regular updating.

In a report prepared for the National Trust after Hurricane Hugo and the Loma Prieta earthquake, Ben Boozer of the South Carolina Main Street Program listed a number of considerations that provide a basis for planning for almost any catastrophe:

DISASTER PLANNING PRINCIPLES

Plan for the worst. All planning should assume a worst-case scenario. This strategy will improve the probability of planning for the disaster that actually does occur.

Plan for all possible circumstances. In the case of Hurricane Hugo, emergency plans failed to anticipate the heavy rains that followed two days later. In California, earthquake-response plans for historic structures did not exist in many localities. After-effects such as flooding, drainage, rain and fire all should be considered in developing plans.

Assume no outside help or resources. The plan should include a directory of outside resources but must provide also for total self-reliance. Remember that transportation of people and supplies may be difficult or impossible.

Plan for the aftermath. While the worst may occur during and immediately after a disaster, other problems may arise a week or two later. For example, after Hurricane Hugo and the Loma Prieta earthquake some areas were without water and electricity for weeks.

Determine who can help and what they can do. Plans should include possible work schedules. Specific task outlines should be developed.

Keep telephone numbers current. Periodic updates of plan telephone numbers, or "call-up lists," are essential. A disaster phone list must include utilities, public safety agencies, key volunteers, key national or out-of-state contacts and other resources.

Plans should always list stockpile contents and locations. Basic supplies always should be kept at hand. Water, food, clean-up supplies, emergency power gear and protective materials should be available, either on site or close by.

Develop a list of craftspersons and trades workers. As part of the regular maintenance program, prepare a list of people potentially available for disaster repair and clean-up. Make sure that they are also aware of the disaster preparedness plan's contents and that their locations and telephone numbers are listed in it.

Ensure adequate training. Staff and key volunteers must be trained. They must know what is expected of them, especially because they may face personal crises and travel difficulties.

Update and train periodically. Historical organizations and sites constantly change. The plan must change with them, and staff must be familiar with it.

Stress ongoing maintenance. Well-maintained historic structures fare better in a disaster. Develop and adhere to a regular maintenance program.

Relocate the most valuable items in an emergency if time permits. Historic property managers may want to work out cross-storage agreements with managers in other regions, assuming secure transportation can be arranged. If an impending disaster is less serious, one-of-a-kind collection items and furniture may simply be moved to upper floors. Paintings can be stored in closets. Library catalogs can be shrouded in plastic or relocated. The key is identifying which ones to specially protect, and when, where and under what circumstances to move them.

Check insurance policies regularly. Become familiar with what catastrophes they cover and update replacement costs as necessary. Periodically reconsider the appropriateness of the deductibles provided by the policies.

Do not ignore financial planning. A natural disaster may create a financial one. If possible, build up reserves in every budget. Disruption of business in subsequent months — and years — can cause major financial damage.

Address normal programmatic activity in disaster planning. The preparedness plan should present strategies for getting back to normal. For historic places open to the public, plans should include promotional campaigns stressing "business as usual" and postdisaster fund-raising efforts. Plans can be developed to keep the public from unsafe buildings without closing off an entire street — or demolishing historic structures simply to reopen a commercial area.

COMPONENTS OF A DISASTER PLAN

The contents of preparedness plans will differ for different situations: from individual historic places (large, small, public, private) to networks of sites, from museums to private homes, from cities and counties to states. But the general components of such plans can be synthesized into models that preservationists and public officials can adapt to their specific local needs. A typical preparedness plan, as suggested by John Hunter of the National Park Service, is organized as follows:

Introduction and statement of purpose. Why the plan was written, who developed it, how it is kept current.

Authority. Who directed the plan's preparation (e.g., mayor, board of trustees) and who will implement it (e.g., planning coordinator, executive director). Designation of person to be responsible during emergencies.

Scope of the plan. Events planned for: in priority order, each type of emergency, likely occurrences and expected impacts.

Locations planned for: indications of which sites are covered by the plan and under what circumstances. Alternatively, separate plans can be developed for multiple sites.

Relationship of the plan to other documents: statement of how supplemental plans (for example, fire protection, security and health emergency) within an institution relate, as well as how this plan relates to local and state civil defense or disaster plans.

Emergency procedures. May be divided into disaster avoidance, mitigation, response and recovery. Tells exactly what should be done to prevent, cope with and recover from emergencies. Describes who puts the plan into action, under what circumstances, how responses are to be implemented. Preferably, addresses each potential disaster in terms of before, during and after.

Appendixes. Information specific to each need that may be subject to frequent change and thus require periodic updating. Typical examples include:

1 Staffing and organizational charts

2 Organizational chart of relationships to other institutions and public disaster agencies

3 Chart of disaster control responsibilities

4 Key personnel responsible for executing the plan, with names, titles, addresses, office and home telephone numbers, and duties

5 Instructions for contacting outside personnel and organizations, such as police, fire, utilities, hospitals, repair companies, insurance agents, technical experts, with notes about why each is listed and services offered and contingency plans in the event that communications lines are down or overloaded

6 Maps and floor plans of individual sites showing emergency evacuation routes, locations of utility cutoffs, telephone closets, fire-fighting equipment, emergency supplies and related items

7 Inventories of important objects, records and other valuable assets, with priorities for their protection; include a floor plan for quick location of assets in an emergency (omit the floor plan in backup copies stored outside the building so that it does not become a burglar's "shopping list")

8 Summary of arrangements to relocate or evacuate collections, with persons to contact and alternative locations

9 Instructions for emergency operation of utilities and building systems

10 List of emergency supplies and equipment, noting where they are located, what they are to be used for and who is to use them; include information on borrowing or buying additional items

11 Information on who is to provide transportation for emergency supplies, equipment and personnel, including alternative arrangements

12 Names and telephone numbers of experts such as conservators, architects and contractors who can be called on for advice and assistance

13 Glossary of terms used in the plan, so that everyone speaks the same language in an emergency

Disaster plans are best kept in a ring binder, advises Hunter. The original should be placed in a safe, fire-resistant and waterproof location, together with any supplementary information needed in an emergency. Copies of the plan should be given to all key persons responsible for executing it. The emergency coordinator should have a copy nearby at all times to update information as needed. If the plan covers more than one site, copies should be placed at each site.

Every site or agency responsible for disaster planning should designate an alternate work site in case of an emergency. Preservationists also should develop plans for how they will accept the offers of volunteers and work with the many well-meaning people who will flood in to help after a disaster.

When developing a disaster plan, keep in mind that all of the checklists and suggested courses of action are only guides — they should not stifle initiative, collaboration or common sense.

DISASTER PREPAREDNESS PLAN

Reprinted here is the disaster preparedness plan of Ashton Villa (1859), a historic house museum owned and operated by the Galveston Historical Foundation and located on the extremely vulnerable barrier island of Galveston, Tex. This plan, revised in June 1990, is a simple, straightforward document whose components can be adapted by other historic sites as well as preservationists with a variety of other institutions:

Plan for Ashton Villa

The Ashton Villa Disaster Preparedness Plan focuses on hurricane preparedness and recovery. The decision to concentrate on hurricanes was based on the extreme vulnerability of Galveston Island to these awesome storms.

The hurricane is the most destructive weather phenomenon known to man. Those affecting the Texas Gulf Coast can occur any time between June and October, and can cover hundreds of thousands of square miles. Damages can be expected from several sources: wind, sustained or gusting from 75 to 200 miles per hour; the storm surge, a huge dome of water causing inundation (usually responsible for the greatest loss of life and destruction of property); and deteriorated conditions during the storm's aftermath.

The National Weather Service advises that Ashton Villa, at just nine feet above sea level, can anticipate flooding if tides rise above six feet. Interstate highway 45, the major escape route from the city, will be flooded and closed after a four-foot tide, therefore making early preparations and evacuation vital.

The Ashton Villa Disaster Preparedness Plan addresses the issues of expected flooding; possible leakage of water from the roof, windows and doors; probable damage from flying objects during high winds; and possible staff disorganization both before and after a hurricane. The plan is composed of four basic parts:

I Assessment of Vulnerability
II Prestorm Preparations
III Recovery
IV Appendixes of Vital Information (subject to changes as needed)

By committing the Ashton Villa Disaster Preparedness Plan to writing, reduction in the time needed to implement it is anticipated. With emergency instructions defined, the impact of such a disaster should be lessened. Detailed instruction and checklists are included in the plan and responsibilities have been designated. The Ashton Villa Disaster Preparedness Plan is reviewed by May of each year, before the start of the hurricane season.

I Assessment of Vulnerability

A Vulnerability Checklist (for monthly review during hurricane season). Responsibility of Ashton Villa director.

    1 Roof in good repair.

    2 Shutters securely hinged.

    3 Shutter locks in good working condition.

    4 Trees trimmed and healthy.

    5 Staff aware of recommended procedures outlined in this plan.

    6 Emergency supplies available and in working condition.

B Vulnerability Assessment (when storm is imminent). Responsibility of Ashton Villa director.

In order to allow ample time for staff evacuation from the Island, should it be advisable, and in order to allow adequate preparation time, the director must assess the intensity of the impending storm and the time projected for landfall. Having made this analysis, the director must make a decision regarding starting time, extent of protection needed and completion time for the procedures outlined in this plan.

The Ashton Villa director is first in responsibility and has final authority in this matter. In the director's absence, the assistant director has this responsibility.

II Prestorm Preparations

A List of Museum Assets to Be Protected

Asset	Responsibility
Staff	Director
Volunteers	Head Tour Guide
Visitors	Head Tour Guide
Clients	Assistant Director
Administrative Offices	Director/Assistant Director
Archeological Area/Gift Shop/ Theater/Exterior/Ballroom	Head Cashier
Collection	Director/Assistant Director/Museum Site Assistant
Apartment	Tenant

B Materials

1 A file containing written materials relating to Gulf Coast hurricanes is available to staff and volunteers. The file, labeled "Hurricanes," is kept in a fireproof file cabinet in the center office. Responsibility of assistant director.

2 Weather radio is kept in safe in administrative office. Responsibility of assistant director.

3 Phone rosters and other information subject to change and update are attached to this plan in the form of appendices. Responsibility of director.

4 Emergency materials related to the security of collection, museum interior and building exterior are stored in a designated area on the third floor. Responsibility of museum site assistant.

5 Shutters for administrative office windows are stored in gift shop closet (upper half—accessible by narrow, high doors on east wall, south side of room). Responsibility of assistant director.

C Storage Space for Collection

If the severity of the storm is judged by the director to warrant removal or storage of the collection, artifacts original to Ashton Villa will be given first consideration. Extensive storage is generally unwarranted. The director will decide on extent of security. Should storage be necessary, Appendix 8 will serve as a guide. Appendix 7 is a list of original Ashton Villa artifacts and their exhibited locations.

Director's Responsibilities Checklist

1 Make decisions regarding extent of vulnerability, immediacy of need and timetable for starting and completing process.

2 Direct all disaster plan activities.

3 Communicate with Galveston Historical Foundation headquarters associate director for museums, and executive director, regarding plans.

4 Advise associate director for museums if Galveston Historical Foundation staff support is needed.

5 Relate decisions regarding plans to Ashton Villa Committee chairman.

6 Inform of closing (see telephone numbers in Appendix 1):
Ashton Villa Gardener
Ashton Villa Museum Site Assistant
Ashton Villa Custodian
ADT (fire alarm system company)
Alert Alarms (security alarm system company)
Apartment tenant
Galveston Police Department

7 Check appointment calendar and advise where necessary.

8 Store active files in fireproof file cabinet.

9 Prepare a final report for Ashton Villa Committee file.

Make three copies of this checklist, include with other checklists in packets to: Ashton Villa Committee chairman, Galveston Historical Foundation executive director and Galveston Historical Foundation associate director for museums.

Make final check of site security.

_____

Director's Signature   Date

Assistant Director's Responsibilities Checklist

1 Telephone to inform of closing:
Galveston Historical Foundation Public Relations Department
Strand Visitors Center
Convention and Visitors Bureau
Elissa
Williams Home
All scheduled group tours
All paid tour guides
All volunteers
All ballroom renters affected by closing

2 Secure kitchen and gift shop (if cashier and head tour guide are on the job they may assume the kitchen and gift shop preparatory duties):
Clear kitchen cabinets and lock.
Unplug all equipment/appliances; store smaller ones in cabinets.
Store cash register on kitchen cabinet and cover with plastic.
Protect projectors by wrapping in plastic bags and store in kitchen cabinets.
Turn off all heat/air conditioning in carriage house and kitchen.
Clear gift shop of all items and store off the ground, if possible.
Clear brochure racks and store on high shelf in cashier's closet.

3 Secure administrative offices:
Unplug all equipment/appliances and cover with plastic.
Move computer and related equipment away from windows and cover with plastic.
Store architectural renderings and floor plans in entrance hall closet.
Clear all surfaces, storing as much as possible in desk drawers or cabinets; secure other materials in plastic bags and place under desks.
Tape supply cabinets and file drawers shut.

4 Miscellaneous duties:
Balance all cash, keeping $50.00. Deposit all other cash, checks and/or credit card vouchers.
File all active files, letters and attendance records in fireproof cabinet.
Take mail to post office.
Secure docent information and master roster.
Secure all information regarding tours and rentals in fireproof cabinet.

Make three copies of this completed checklist. Give original and a copy to director; place a copy in safe.

Assistant Director's Signature   Date

Museum Site Assistant's Responsibilities Checklist

1 Confer with director regarding extent of protection needed and implement storage/security plans accordingly.

2 Hook and tie all shutters on main house, ballroom, carriage house/tack room, administrative offices.

3 Tie up all draperies on first floor of museum.

4 Unplug all equipment/appliances.

5 All furniture will be moved into the center of each room, away from windows and skylights. In case of severe storm probability, furniture may be covered with plastic for further protection.

6 All artwork on walls will remain on walls unless there is probability of severe storm. Small paintings in close proximity to windows may be taken down and covered with plastic. Large paintings may be covered with plastic. Original Brown paintings will be the first to be taken down and stored in closets as near to their exhibited location as possible.

Make three copies of this checklist. Give original and a copy to the director, and keep a copy for the files.

Museum Site Assistant's Signature   Date

III Recovery

A. Postdisaster Communication

1 Contact Galveston Historical Foundation executive director and/or museum director as soon as possible regarding status of property.

2 Appendix 1 lists staff telephone numbers including alternate numbers for contacting the Ashton Villa director.

B Insurance

1 Policies are kept at and administered from the Galveston Historical Foundation's offices at 2016 Strand.

2 Insurance company is listed under recovery contacts. See Appendix 1.

3 A preliminary damage list must be formulated as quickly as possible and delivered to the insurance company. Responsibility of the director.

4 Only necessary temporary repairs should be made. Wait for insurance adjuster before making permanent repairs.

C Collection

If collection is damaged, immediately contact consultants listed in Appendix 1.

D Miscellaneous

1 Assess degree of danger.

2 Assess degree of damage.

3 Select methods.

4 Assign duties.

5 Inform Galveston Historical Foundation offices: executive director, associate director of museums and public relations director.

E Critique

1 Reassess vulnerability, methods of preparation and recovery.

2 Send written report to: Galveston Historical Foundation board of directors, c/o executive director, Ashton Villa Committee and Texas Historical Commission.

3 Revise Ashton Villa Disaster Preparedness Plan as needed.

IV Table of Contents of Appendixes

Reducing Vulnerability

According to California consulting engineer Melvyn Green, reducing vulnerability to disasters involves the following five steps:

1 Identifying specific hazards

2 Determining goals

3 Selecting and setting appropriate standards

4 Evaluating structures and their contents

5 Taking mitigating action to correct deficiencies

Identifying hazards. Historic places face the common natural hazards covered in this book — earthquakes, hurricanes, tornadoes, floods and fires — as well as even more likely threats such as burst pipes, unsafe wiring and vandalism.

Determining goals. Broad preparedness goals will be, in priority order, to protect lives, protect historic structures and protect collections. Historic buildings that are well maintained and in compliance with applicable building codes are less likely to endanger occupants or passersby and more likely to survive a disaster. For collections, preparing the disaster plan itself may, by setting priorities, provide the most protection to objects valued most highly.

Setting standards. A variety of legal regulations apply to buildings, historic and otherwise. More stringent standards may be adopted, to strengthen a structure beyond the letter of the codes, but minimum requirements will be found in the following local legal codes:

1 Construction regulations: building codes, electrical codes, plumbing codes, mechanical codes and health codes

2 Maintenance regulations: fire prevention codes, health codes, abatement codes for dangerous buildings and property maintenance codes

3 Retroactive regulations: fire safety — involving stairways, sprinklers and smoke detectors — and seismic — involving unreinforced masonry structures and walls and elevators

Evaluating structures and contents. Once standards are selected, and approved if necessary by an appropriate governing board, it is time to investigate the structure and compare its condition with the regulations. This means giving a historic building and its setting a complete physical examination, from roof to foundation and everything in between, together with the surrounding landscape.

The following checklist outlines areas that should be inspected periodically, as part of routine maintenance, not just in preparation for disasters:

Foundation and Masonry

1 Check foundations, masonry, basements and exterior walls for seepage and condensation problems.

2 Check basements for leakage after wet weather.

3 Check foundation walls, steps, retaining walls, walks, patios, driveways, garage floors and similar areas for settling, cracks, heaving and crumbling.

4 Ensure that the foundation is attached to the structure.

5 Check chimneys for deteriorated caps and loose and missing mortar.

6 Make sure that landscape grading slopes away from foundation walls.

Unreinforced Masonry Buildings

1 Securely attach parts and architectural decoration. Parapets can be braced, unanchored veneer can be anchored, individual loose bricks can be reset in new mortar.

2 Anchor walls to the floor and roof framing using steel or other reinforcements.

3 If diaphragms cannot be strengthened, install partitions to supplement them.

4 Analyze shear walls to determine if they need additional strengthening to avoid cracking or lateral drift.

5 If necessary, strengthen "soft" first stories and basements, where internal walls have been opened up (whether by original design or alteration) to provide for commercial space and parking.

Roofs and Gutters

1 Look for damaged, loose or missing shingles or tiles. Check flat roofs for blisters, cracks and other damage. Is there any sagging that might indicate previous damage covered with a new roof?

2 Check for leaking, misaligned or damaged gutters, downspouts, straps, gutter guards and strainers. All water-carrying elements should be clean and free from obstructions. Downspouts should direct water away from the structure.

3 Remove tree limbs on or over roofs that may be a clear hazard.

4 Be sure that flashings around roof stacks, vents, skylights and chimneys are not sources of leakage.

5 Remove nests that may clog vents, louvers and chimneys.

6 Rehabilitate any decayed fascias, soffits and other trim material, and ornamentation.

7 Refasten any decayed or inadequately fastened masonry and stone ornamentation.

Exterior Walls

1 Repaint surfaces that have flaked, as they may fail and allow water incursion.

2 Check any siding, shingles, trim and ornamentation for damage, looseness, warping and decay.

3 Repair cracks and missing or broken mortar in masonry buildings.

Doors and Windows

1 Check caulking and decay around doors, windows, corner boards, joints and similar areas.

2 Check glazing around window panes.

3 Check weatherstripping.

Utilities

1 Know the location of the main electrical panel. Make sure that each circuit is labeled correctly. Know how to turn off the power.

2 Know the location of the main disconnection switch for the heating and hot water systems, as well as how to operate it.

3 Know the condition of the plumbing and the location of the main water disconnection valve.

4 Have utility systems professionally inspected periodically.

Landscapes

1 Know the condition of trees and shrubbery.

2 Remove dead limbs.

3 Keep plantings trimmed near foundation lines and roofs.

Overall

1 Closely examine the entire structure for general stability.

2 In daylight from afar, perhaps with binoculars, determine whether the structure seems true. Are window and door openings also true?

3 From up close, use a plumb bob or carpenter's level to check for basic structural problems.

Correcting deficiencies. Beyond good maintenance practices, correcting perceived deficiencies in historic structures to prepare them for disasters involves some weighing and balancing: What is an acceptable risk? Which changes can be made without altering the historical character of a building or district? Which alterations are cost effective?

UNREINFORCED MASONRY BUILDINGS

Unreinforced masonry buildings, the likeliest victims of an earthquake, are among the most problematic issues in disaster preparedness—there are so many of them, it is expensive to retrofit them, and retrofitting can bring serious alterations in the appearance and fabric of a historic structure. Cities such as Los Angeles and San Francisco have been studying ways of increasing the safety of these buildings. Alternatives for citywide action range from making no requirement for seismic reinforcement to encouraging and assisting voluntary reinforcement; requiring that owners connect floors to walls and take other steps to prevent walls from falling out; creating an ordinance requiring owners to complete basic minimum upgrades; and requiring reinforcement only when occupancy is increased. Also under study are mitigating measures such as providing low-cost financing, incentives and relocation from endangered buildings. To protect historic structures and low-income housing, preservationists and others are working to ensure that wide-scale demolition and unsympathetic alterations are discouraged.

FIRE PREVENTION

Fires are among the most preventable of disasters. According to the noted British restoration architect Sir Bernard M. Feilden, two objectives should govern emergency preparedness for fires: (1) protecting lives by ensuring that occupants can get out quickly if one starts, and (2) retrofitting buildings in such a way that fires can be contained to a portion of the structure. The first objective is the purpose of fire codes. The second can, if successful, help spare historic buildings and collections and also contribute to the primary goal of saving lives. In historic buildings open to the public, fire safety plans and modifications are of special importance because old and historic structures may not have been designed with fire protection and mitigation in mind.

Feilden divides the second objective into three parts: (1) to prevent the outbreak of fire, (2) to minimize the effects of a fire by preventing its spread (passive fire protection), and (3) to allow the fire to be fought efficiently with minimum damage to house or museum contents (active fire protection). These steps may involve:

1 Devising protected escape routes, including application of fire-retardant materials and coatings

2 Enclosing staircases and installing fire doors where they will not adversely affect a building's historical appearance

3 Installing alarms, detectors, extinguishers, sprinklers, emergency lighting and similar safety features

4 Compartmentalizing a structure by installing fire blocks in ceilings, floors and walls (ventilation grilles and ductwork may provide a ready pathway for fire to spread)

5 Dividing open attics and roof spaces into more manageable areas by installing fire-resistant walls

Fire drills are a good idea for the occupants of all structures, but they may be particularly important for those who spend time in historic buildings. They should be practiced regularly. For historic buildings open to the public, appropriate fire department officials should be consulted about fire preparedness, in particular before any structural or other modifications are undertaken that may affect fire worthiness.

Preparing for the Event

To cope with a natural disaster or any potential emergency, appropriate supplies and equipment should be available. The list printed below, developed by John Hunter of the National Park Service, is not exhaustive; however, it is probably much more comprehensive than any particular disaster preparedness plan need contemplate. One caveat: emergency supplies and equipment kept on hand should be considered part of the disaster preparedness plan. Some of them deteriorate with time. Others require instructional manuals for proper and safe usage. And be especially careful to read the labels and manuals before using, because some chemicals can form deadly compounds when mixed.

EMERGENCY SUPPLIES AND EQUIPMENT

Debris Removal and Cleanup
Low-sudsing detergents
Bleaches
Sanitizers (such as chloride of lime or high-test hypochlorite)
Fungicides
Disinfectants
Ammonia
Scouring powders or other cleaners
Brooms
Dustpans
Mops, mop buckets and wringers
Paper towels
Scoops and shovels

Scrub brushes
Sponges and rags
Buckets
Washtubs
Water hoses and nozzles
Containers for garbage
Wet/dry vacuum cleaner with accessories

Demolition, Repairs and Rescue
(Power tools may not be usable without a portable generator.)
Hammers (claw and machinist's)
Wrenches (pipe, channel lock and vise grips, various sizes)

Better Late Than Never

About 10 days before Hurricane Hugo hit Charleston, the president of the College of Charleston, Harry M. Lightsey, Jr., became alerted that a storm was gathering strength in the Atlantic. He took the emergency plan from the files and passed it along to the senior staff, who decided a day later that it was not going to work.

Our group of 12, including the maintenance director and security chief, asked, "What's likely to happen?" The answer: "Well, it's going to blow off some roofs." We asked: "What does that mean?" The answer: "Well, it means we're going to have to get some people up here covering them up." We needed lathing and a lot of plastic. We had none.

Thus, eight days before the hurricane, the college began a flurry of activity. We bought plastic, lathing and generators. We picked up and stored benches from around the campus. We set up a communications center in our National Register–listed administration building. We set up an emergency shelter for the neighborhood. We arranged for a nurse and medical intern. And on the day before the storm, the college's baseball team moved books and computers up from the library's ground floor. One thing we neglected to plan for was tree damage: we needed chain saws. But at 7 a.m. on the day after the storm, we had people on roofs, putting down plastic.

The campus was the first place in Charleston that was cleaned and ready for normal operations — for two reasons: (1) the leadership provided by President Lightsey, and (2) our plan, which, even if prepared to some degree at the last minute, involved every constituency on campus.

Conrad D. Festa, Senior Vice President for Academic Affairs
College of Charleston

Pliers (adjustable, lineman's and needle nose, various sizes)

Screwdrivers (straight blade and Phillips, various sizes)

Tools for tamper-resistant screws and bolts

Wood saws

Metal saw with blades

Utility knife with blades

Wire cutters with insulated handles

Tin snips

Pipe cutter and threaders

Bolt cutter

Hand drill with bits

Pry bar or crowbar

Axes, including firefighter's axe

Dollies or handcarts

Sledgehammer

Pit-cover hook

Folding rule or retractable tape measure

Hydrant and post indicator valve wrenches (for sprinkler or standpipe systems)

Staple gun and staples

Ladders and stools

Rope

Three-ton hydraulic jack

Block and tackle

Construction Materials

Plywood (for covering or replacing broken windows)

Dimensional lumber

Nails, screws and assorted fasteners

Tapes (masking, duct, electrician's)

Glue

Twine and rope

Plastic sheeting (for protection against leaks and splashes)

Binding wire

Emergency Equipment

Gasoline-powered electrical generator

Portable lights (if power or generator is available)

Emergency lights with extra batteries

Fire extinguishers (ABC type)

Battery-operated radio(s) with extra batteries

Walkie-talkie radios with extra batteries

CB radio with extra batteries

Portable public address system or bullhorn

Geiger counter and dosimeters

Gas masks with extra canisters

Air breathers with extra oxygen masks

Resuscitation equipment

Power water pump with appropriate hoses and fittings

Heavy-duty extension cords, preferably equipped with ground fault interrupters

Personal Equipment and Supplies

(Some may be provided by the individuals who are to use them.)

Protective clothing

Rubber boots or waders

Rubber gloves

Hard hats

Rubber lab aprons

Protective masks and goggles and safety glasses

First-aid kits

Food and food preparation equipment

Potable water

Sanitation facilities

Changes of clothing

Sleeping bags, blankets and pillows

Miscellaneous Supplies

Boxes; plastic milk crates

Sealing and strapping tape

Packing materials (tissue paper, clean newsprint, plastic bubble pack, extruded foam)

Marking pens

Insecticides and rodenticides

Hand or compressed air sprayers

Miscellaneous Equipment

Portable fans

Space heaters

Portable dehumidifiers

Hygrometers and moisture meters

Photographic equipment (35mm camera, lenses, accessories such as film and batteries)

Essential office equipment (manual typewriter, pocket calculator, pencil sharpener, stapler, rulers)

Essential stationery and blank forms

Conservation Supplies and Equipment

Polyester (Mylar) and polyethylene film

Newsprint (unprinted)

Polyethylene bags in various sizes

Plastic garbage bags

Thymol

Ethanol

Acetone

Industrial denatured alcohol

Dry ice

White blotter paper

Various sizes of thick glass or smooth Masonite (for flattening paper)

Weights

Japanese tissue

Freezer or wax paper

Towels or clean rags

Clothes pins, preferably plastic

Scissors

Sharp drafting knives

Water displacement compound

Waxes and dressings

This list of supplies and equipment was developed with a focus on both the historic structure and its contents. Bear in mind that many of these items will already be on hand. The unfortunate possibility, however, is that when disaster occurs the supply of a critical item will be on order. Adopting a warehouse mentality is appropriate: rotate stock, and keep the inventory up-to-date.

PREPAREDNESS CHECKLIST

In Oklahoma the predominant natural threats to historic places come from quick-developing emergencies such as tornadoes, fires and floods. Daily as well as periodic inspection regimens thus are crucial. The following items are highlighted in a disaster preparedness checklist developed by an Oklahoma Conservation Congress representative and published by the Oklahoma Museums Association and Oklahoma Historical Society:

Daily Procedures

1 Locks on doors and windows secure and all keys accounted for

2 No pipes, faucets, toilets or air-conditioning units leaking

3 Electrical equipment unplugged and no frayed wiring in evidence

4 No signs of structural damage

5 No burning materials in ashtrays and wastebaskets

Periodic Procedures   *Date Checked*

1   Emergency numbers are accurate and posted by every phone   _____

2   Most recent inspection by fire department   _____

3   Fire extinguishers operable   _____

4   Smoke alarms operable   _____

5   Sprinkler system operable   _____

6   Water detectors operable   _____

7   Halon system operable   _____

8   Public address system operable   _____

9   Operable flashlights placed in every department and civil
defense shelter   _____

10 Transistor radio operable   _____

11 Staff familiarized (by tour, not just a map) with locations of fire extinguishers,
flashlights, radio, civil defense shelter and how to reach members of the in-house
disaster recovery team   _____

12 Most recent fire drill   _____

13 Most recent civil defense drill   _____

14 Most recent tornado drill   _____

Insurance: Are You in Good Hands?

Another critical aspect of disaster planning is insurance, for owners of private historic buildings as well as for those who manage public structures. Adequate coverage for all disaster circumstances may be difficult to obtain. Earthquake insurance, for example, is expensive, and some carriers will not insure brick buildings. Deductibles may be high, in the 10 to 20 percent range, and are based on property value, not damages. Business interruption losses and retrofitting to meet safety codes may not be reimbursable unless additional disaster insurance is carried.

An assessment of coverage should be made on a regular basis, and disaster planning should make note of where policies are kept and how to contact the insurance agent or company. Insurance experts caution that claims for structures and landscapes must be backed up by written appraisals and documentation. If owners and managers have followed correct preservation procedures, documenting their historic assets thoroughly before a disaster as part of emergency preparedness and immediately after a disaster as part of damage assessment, they should be well prepared to file insurance claims.

Questions to ask the insurance company or agent before a disaster include:

1 How much insurance does the property, institution or organization have?

2 Are all of the objects in the building or collection covered? Are there exclusions? Is the building covered? The landscape?

3 Exactly what circumstances are covered in a disaster?

4 What records are needed for claims? Does a copy exist off the premises?

5 What about records of the condition of the structure or its contents? What documentation will the insurance company require about predisaster conditions, and what will it cost to restore them?

6 If a disaster occurs, can recovery begin immediately, or must an insurance agent or company representative first inspect the damage? (Immediate access is essential for historic structures and their collections and may require cooperation from police and fire departments.)

7 When will recovery funds be available?

8 Who makes the decision whether to restore or replace?

9 How much time is allowed to file a final claim?

For most owners and managers of historic properties, these questions are difficult to answer. In the first place, they are almost impossible to answer completely, and they suggest the complexity inherent in comprehensive disaster planning. For example, which objects must be protected at all costs? What part of the structure is truly irreplaceable? Is it possible to insure something that is one of a kind? If it is priceless, how can one set a value on it?

"Replacement" versus "restoration" coverage. The traditional homeowners insurance policy probably will be insufficient for a private historic structure. It generally provides a dollar amount of coverage to reconstruct damaged areas using "commonly or readily available" materials and mentions nothing about the quality of craftsmanship. Newer, "deluxe" homeowners policies offer what is called replacement-cost insurance that promises to cover use of materials and workmanship of "like and kind quality," although this language still does not mean restoration of the damaged premises.

To assess damages, an experienced appraiser or estimator is important. In the aftermath of Hurricane Hugo, many owners of historic houses discovered halfway or three-quarters of the way through restoration that the insurance settlement had run out — but because settlement had taken place, they had no recourse with the insurance company.

Precautions may reduce premiums. Fire extinguishers, smoke and heat detectors, water detectors, sprinklers, fire alarms and written disaster preparedness plans all can have an effect on costs.

Collections. Collections require special consideration, and they are almost always insured under separate policies from structures and other personal property, such as office equipment. Policies may cover either specific items or a total amount for damage to the collection, or parts of it; they also may be written for specific hazards or "all perils." The broadest possible coverage probably is the best bet, including protection for borrowed collections and transportation of collection items. Bear in mind that collections often are undervalued; their rarity and the cost of appropriate conservation may not be considered when setting coverage limits. A written record of a structure's contents will be required for any insurance settlement.

Landscapes. Landscapes are particularly problematical to insure, and are often less protected. Hurricane Hugo's enormous destruction to plant resources was a case in point. Many homeowners found that their insurance covered removing fallen trees, but not their replacement. Regular homeowners policies provide landscape coverage limited to a set amount, such as five percent of the coverage on the structure, or contain limitations on the coverage for each tree or landscape plant. Policies may also insure only for sudden and extraordinary events — an earthquake would certainly qualify, but not necessarily storm winds.

Earthquakes. Earthquake coverage is another special case. California law requires insurance companies to offer it in writing, but only a small percentage of homeowners carry it. Such coverage is usually offered with a large deductible, typically five to 15 percent of policy limits. Damage caused by tremors may also be covered under ordinary insurance policies, as when a broken gas line leads to fire damage.

Additional coverage. Other items that should be addressed include loss of income, liability exposure, workers compensation, and trustees' and officers' liability.

Insurance pools. Modeled after the federal flood insurance program, several states have established insurance pools to ensure that coverage is available in high-risk, disaster-prone areas. Texas has a windstorm pool for its coastal areas that are vulnerable to hurricanes and other windstorms. All insurance companies in the state are required to participate so that all owners can purchase coverage at regulated rates designed to be reasonable and affordable. The state created set zones that have specific rates. Improvements such as the seawall in Galveston help reduce a zone's rates. After the Loma Prieta earthquake, the California legislature established a similar disaster insurance program. Through its rates, it encourages seismic retrofitting — another incentive to upgrade existing buildings.

Public Education

What should preservationists and public officials do to make sure that people know how to act before and during disasters to save historic buildings? Probably the best strategy is to gain the ongoing involvement of the public in preservation—building an ethic of conservation and understanding what it means to care for old buildings. Educating the public on how to protect old buildings during natural disasters should be an integral part of the preservation process. As recent events underscore, historic buildings may suffer doubly when disaster hits. After Loma Prieta, old structures faced not only the shaking of the earth, but also the rush to "do something" immediately.

BUILDING A PRESERVATION ETHIC

Creating a climate in which old buildings will be thought about during disasters begins with a few basic steps:

1 Develop ongoing support for preservation values that will carry over to any emergency.

2 Encourage owners of old buildings, public and private, to have their own emergency plans.

3 Help property owners appropriately retrofit buildings to survive disasters.

4 Develop a concern for continual routine maintenance to give old structures and landscapes an edge in surviving disasters. To this end, sponsor seminars and produce publications for property owners.

5 Distribute practical information on surviving a disaster—from emergency supplies to advice on how, what and when to rehabilitate afterward.

6 Compile lists of architects, contractors, conservators and other experts qualified to work on old structures and share them with owners after an emergency. Prepare similar lists of suppliers of appropriate materials.

7 Know what disaster funding sources may be available and provide this information as needed.

8 Be prepared to react quickly to reassure the public during a disaster, by working with other preservationists and public officials—have a plan, an alternate work site and ways of channeling volunteers.

9 Complete needed historic resource surveys as soon as possible so that everyone will know where the historic places are.

10 Seek passage of local preservation ordinances to safeguard historic sites now, before a disaster strikes; include provisions for emergency situations.

A central strategy in any public outreach or disaster education effort is to use the media. Coverage by local newspapers and radio and television stations is among the most effective ways of gaining attention and support for preservation—from homeowners to elected officials—if carried out thoughtfully.

Consistency. The first rule in achieving media attention, both before and during a disaster, is to designate one, and only one, staff member to be in charge of media relations. Telling more than one version of the same event greatly dilutes its impact on the public. This does not mean that members of a board of directors, or a historic site manager, cannot talk to the press. It does mean that the person in charge of media relations must know who is going to say what, and when. The point is to make sure that the voice of the institution is heard, and that it is consistent.

Continuity. An equally important reason for designating a media representative is continuity. The person who has developed long-term relationships with reporters and producers is much more likely to succeed in telling the story during a disaster. The media officer also will have had the opportunity to prepare, by having at hand names and telephone numbers of appropriate preservation leaders and government officials, knowledge of local ordinances and legislation on preservation, names and telephone numbers of good interview subjects, plans for recovery; and names and addresses of relevant local historic places. The media representative will also follow up when stories and television coverage happen, thanking the reporter or producer, and making sure that elected officials receive copies or transcripts.

FAIR-WEATHER PLANNING

Cities that have weathered natural disasters in the past can share their hardwon lessons. Galveston, Tex., is one such place, a narrow barrier island so low that the sea does not have to rise much to inundate it. The island, now home to 65,000 residents and many visitors to historic sites such as Ashton Villa, was devastated in 1900 by what has been called the deadliest natural disaster in American history. At least 6,000 persons died, and half of its houses were swept away.

Hurricanes continue to batter Galveston, but now the city is about as prepared as it can be. Following Hurricane Alicia in 1983, new Mayor Jan Coggeshall helped launch a public education program that has been called a model for the nation. Its motto, given Galveston's vulnerable physiognomy, is "Don't Be Late. Evacuate." This theme is drummed into residents' consciousness throughout the year, culminating in a town meeting devoted especially to disaster preparedness each spring, before the start of hurricane season. Like an old-time town fair, the meeting generates excitement in its posters and ad announcements: "Door Prizes! Free Information Materials! Refreshments! Official Re-entry Decals! Hurricane Tracking Charts!" Added to this is an actual fair, the exhibitors being not purveyors of games and cotton candy, but groups such as the Red Cross, hardware and shutter stores, utility companies, safety agencies, FEMA and the National Weather Service. All are there to present "innovative ideas in coping with the hurricane season."

Galveston's pioneering promotional effort has four basic components:

1 Public education. The town meeting, fair and publicity are designed especially for new residents, business managers, teachers, health care workers and tourism managers.

2 Education in schools. Using a video, the city works with school children, sponsoring a bumper sticker contest among other activities.

3 Evacuation program. Stressing the importance of evacuating in advance of a storm, the city makes leaving easier by providing stickers to residents allowing them easy return after the storm warnings are lifted. A special traffic lane gives them priority over sightseers.

4 Regular meetings. The Mayor's Advisory Committee for Emergency Management, which is chaired by the city manager and includes public and private participants, meets monthly.

Galveston also conducts annual drills with its special disaster teams, using different disaster scenarios. Because hurricane season returns each June, the city also conducts a summertime roof check, just to be sure that everything is secured that should be. "For residents, the 1900 storm and Hurricane Carla in 1961 are always in the back of one's mind," says Peter H. Brink, the executive director of the Galveston Historical Foundation for nearly two decades and now the vice president for programs, services and information of the National Trust. "The city government leads a receptive community in developing hurricane preparedness plans, managing storm response and organizing poststorm recovery. The city and its citizens know that their ultimate well-being depends on their own preparedness and follow through."

DURING A DISASTER

Immediate Relief Activities

The historic six-block Pacific Garden Mall in Santa Cruz lost half of its buildings during and after the Loma Prieta quake. To make a record of the damages, the Historic American Buildings Survey used photogrammetry so that it did not have to measure buildings by hand. (John A. Burns, HABS)

THE FUGITIVES who took shelter from

Hurricane Hugo at Lincoln High School in McClellanville, S.C., northeast of Charleston know well the incredible danger and terror a hurricane storm surge can bring. While the still-water surge at McClellanville was measured at "only" 15 to 16 feet above mean sea level (compared to almost 20 feet at Romain Retreat nearer Charleston), to the refugees at Lincoln High it was a close brush with ultimate disaster. When water began to infiltrate the school auditorium, the refugees moved to the stage. When that height proved insufficient, they climbed onto tables to gain another few feet of altitude. Finally, with flood waters continuing to swirl and rise, they punched out the acoustic tiles in the suspended ceiling, then stuffed children into the newly created crawl space below the roof.

Hugo's refugees in Lincoln High were lucky. A higher storm surge might have doomed them, and higher winds could easily have peeled off the flat roof of the auditorium, allowing the building to be quickly washed away. In large part, historic McClellanville survived Hurricane Hugo with great difficulty, and about a quarter of the contributing structures in its National Register historic district sustained major damage.

Although warnings for different kinds of natural disasters vary from no time at all to several days, often actions can be accomplished within severe time constraints to either mitigate damages or facilitate immediate postdisaster steps to protect historic places.

What to Do First: Organizing for the Emergency

Getting ready for a natural disaster is not a special activity. Rather, for everyone responsible for historic places, it should be a regular part of daily business. All of the steps outlined previously, whether taken just before disaster strikes or much earlier as part of a long-term disaster preparedness strategy, have the common goal not of avoiding disaster, but of placing people and objects where disaster is least likely to harm them and putting historic places in the best shape to withstand nature's assault. It should be kept in mind that staff members and volunteers will have their own personal needs in coping with a disaster, so plans must address the fact that not everyone will be able to participate as expected.

EMERGENCY RESPONSE PRINCIPLES

What are the characteristics of a system that will allow preservationists and public officials to organize for an emergency and to begin assessing and recovering from losses? Barclay Jones of Cornell University has identified the following aspects of a such a system:

1 It is able to respond rapidly. Sometimes hours make the difference between protection and further damage to structures and collections.

2 It includes systematic searches for damages.

3 The searches are discriminating, i.e., when damages are found, a quick, preliminary evaluation of threats to a structure is undertaken.

4 The searches are comprehensive, as far as possible, and include written descriptions and lots of photographs. Even seemingly random shots of a damaged structure, or a collection scattered about, can yield valuable clues to aid in recovery and restoration. The search process is crucial and must be done quickly because historic structures and collections may lie wide open to additional damage.

5 Affected sites must be stabilized as much as possible.

6 Concurrent with stabilization, attention should be paid to security. Historic structures and their contents are valuable, even priceless. Objects and ornamentation in particular have a way of disappearing, whether in the zealous sanitation worker's truck or a looter's cache.

7 Mobilization of people and supplies should take place quickly. This process will be speeded by the thorough advance planning previously recommended.

8 Priorities for recovery, determined earlier, should be followed.

9 Participants in recovery efforts must recognize that historic structures and collections require special expertise.

The following sections of this chapter explore these and related issues in greater detail. But, first, a look at one tactical emergency manual will be helpful as an example for others.

Mystic Seaport in Mystic, Conn., is well known as one of the largest historical destinations in New England and one of the most comprehensive historic maritime sites in the United States. Encompassing 17 acres of waterfront buildings, historic houses, ships and a working shipyard, the outdoor museum is open to the public year-round and welcomes a half million visitors annually. Its attractions include historic watercraft such as the square-rigger *Joseph Conrad* and the whaler *Charles W. Morgan*, as well as 400 smaller boats from sloops to steam launches, some of which are afloat. Also on site are several museums exhibiting maritime artifacts, a bookstore and a library. Mystic Seaport, in short, encompasses many components typical of a historic site or district—artifacts, historic and not-so-historic buildings, administrative departments, shops, vessels, shoreline structures, libraries and archives.

Mystic Seaport's emergency manual, a response to the Connecticut coast's most likely threat of hurricanes, is a 112-page checklist and guide to activities during, rather than before, a disaster. It defines the responsibilities, functions and procedures to be followed by the staff in the event of a severe storm. The plan is divided into two broad chapters: first, general information and, second, detailed storm emergency procedures for each of the site's 20 divisions. It includes a series of four steadily escalating action plans based on the increasing likelihood of a major storm:

Condition Watch. The first action level is set by Mystic's planetarium "when there are persuasive indications a severe storm could threaten the Seaport within 48 hours." This declaration sets the plan in motion: a command center is established in the deputy director's office, and the chain of command is used to notify division heads, who begin to carry out the storm preparedness tasks outlined in the plan for their respective departments. Condition Watch is a trigger; it activates the emergency plan.

Condition I. Approximately 36 hours before the storm is predicted to reach Mystic Seaport, the established chain of command, beginning with the director, can declare Condition I: departments continue long lead-time preparations, while the site remains open to visitors, with one exception; the dock master's office closes docks and requests the departure of visiting vessels.

Condition II. Condition II can be instituted when destructive winds and high tides are anticipated within 12 to 18 hours. This action triggers much more serious preparatory steps: the museum is closed, the availability of volunteer staff is determined and allocated according to plan requirements, emergency communications networks are activated, and the command center moves to the planetarium.

Condition III. Condition III begins when the storm is imminent. Command center staff make sure that each department's disaster preparedness checklist is completed, volunteer staff members are redeployed to storm positions, power is turned off and areas are secured. All staff members who have not volunteered for storm duty are dismissed.

Poststorm. When the storm has passed, Mystic Seaport's emergency plan goes into reverse, with the command center evaluating the seriousness of the weather and reducing readiness to Condition II, Condition I and Condition Watch as appropriate.

Mystic's plan also details emergency procedures for each of the historic site's 20 divisions, ranging in size from one to 10 or more pages (an excerpt relating to the public affairs office appears at the end of this chapter). The entire plan emphasizes continuity of communications, not only within the complex, but also with federal, state and local agencies having disaster responsibilities and with the private sector, especially media outlets.

Getting Help

"The crowd at California and Front streets in San Francisco's Financial District stood silent yesterday afternoon," wrote staff writer Carl Nolte in the *San Francisco Chronicle* on November 1, 1989, "as if they were watching a funeral pass by. In a way, they were. Big wrecking claws were taking down what is left of the handsome, six-story Marine Building at 158 California Street, which was irreparably damaged in last month's quake. The building, which had landmark status, was 81 years old."

The above scene was replicated too many times in the aftermath of the Loma Prieta earthquake. Fortunately, it did not happen as often as it could have, because preservationists, private and public, rallied into double overtime to help save threatened historic structures. A number of groups and agencies, ranging from local preservation organizations to volunteer architects and engineers to government employees, coordinated their activities for the most impact, as they did in the Virgin Islands, Puerto Rico and the Carolinas after Hugo. Even San Francisco's editors put in a word: "Be careful with old architecture," admonished the *San Francisco Examiner*, "make sure no more of our architectural heritage is lost than necessary in this period."

WHERE TO GO

During and immediately following a natural disaster, a number of general sources of assistance can be called on, among them:

1 Government: city, county, state and federal (including regional offices)

The Federal Emergency Management Agency has a mandate to assist our civilian population in planning to minimize effects of disasters and in recovery and restoration efforts after a disaster occurs.

A Spanish mission in California, an antebellum mansion in South Carolina and a covered bridge in New Hampshire have at least two things in common: one, they are part of the fabric of America, a reminder of what we were, a vital part of what we are and a benchmark from which we can assess the future; and, two, they are potential victims of earthquakes, hurricanes, floods and fires.

FEMA and the Advisory Council on Historic Preservation are working together to establish guidelines for disasters that will attempt to strike a balance between the actions taken for disaster relief and the needs of historic preservation. There will be continuous and open dialogue with the National Trust for Historic Preservation on these issues as well.

Disaster relief and recovery efforts are subject to a host of state and federal coordination requirements, including the usual requirement to consult with state historic preservation officers regarding proposed actions. Recent history has proven the importance of having contingencies in mind, should a disaster occur.

Clearly, more needs to be done to identify historic properties and develop protection strategies before disaster strikes. This will demand a lot from a public-private partnership of emergency management professionals at all levels of government and the historic preservation community to protect our mutual treasures. Let us hope that we can find some innovative ways to accomplish this goal.

Wallace E. Stickney, Director
Federal Emergency Management Agency

2 Preservation: city preservation agencies, local landmarks and design review boards, statewide, local and other nonprofit preservation organizations, state historic preservation offices, National Trust for Historic Preservation, historic sites

3 Professional: architects, landscape architects, engineers, museum curators, object and art conservators, archivists, librarians, historians, educators, archeologists

4 Construction: contractors, builders, craftspersons, building suppliers, landscapers, haulers

5 Promotional: media, photographers

6 Political: national, state and local legislators, governors, mayors, city and county executives, neighborhood leaders

7 Security: police, firefighters, hospitals, guards

8 Financial: bankers, insurance agents, public funding programs, foundations

9 Volunteers: organization members, trustees, citizens

10 Previous victims: any group or person who has survived a similar disaster and can impart lessons and advice

The best method for ensuring that help will be available when needed is to begin identifying and contacting appropriate providers of assistance as part of the disaster planning process. Some specific sources are listed in the chapter Where to Get Help. The networks identified in Before Disaster Strikes show how organizations can work together. Thorough emergency plans indicate specific names, addresses and telephone numbers to call on when the time comes — because usually there is never time enough when that time arrives.

THE PUBLIC SECTOR

Aid requests to agencies of government charged with preservation and disaster relief should be undertaken without delay. Keep in mind that governments will be focusing first on the health and safety of residents.

Local. The capacity of local government to respond to emergencies will vary from place to place, and particularly from city to rural area. But, in any event, local governments will be the key coordinators of disaster response. Agencies likely to be of help with preservation concerns in a disaster range from the mayor's office and the local disaster preparedness agency to the preservation office, if any, and landmarks commission and design review boards. Local government's chief preservation activity in a disaster will be to see that historic buildings are not demolished without cause and that standard procedures for reviewing work on designated structures continue without inter-

Team Effort in Oakland

After the earthquake, preservationists from various organizations in Oakland came together to form an umbrella action team to respond to the crisis. The Oakland Preservation Assistance Team was made up of representatives of the Oakland Heritage Alliance, East Bay AIA Historic Preservation Committee, Oakland Design Advocates (a group of designers, planners and architects), California Preservation Foundation and National Trust Western Regional Office. Other "at-large" members included attorneys, engineers and local college faculty.

OPAT's goals were to (1) provide owners of historic buildings with technical, engineering, financial and architectural resources; (2) educate the public about the value of restoring old buildings and how to make them seismically safe; (3) encourage the city government to appropriately restore its landmark public buildings; and (4) work with other community groups such as those trying to retain low-income housing, encouraging reuse of old buildings.

In the first hectic weeks OPAT members were in daily communication. The AIA office, centrally located downtown, became the clearinghouse. Earthquake damage had closed the landmark city hall and displaced city staff. Free public workshops were organized to aid repair of wood-frame houses and masonry commercial buildings. Technical and financial aid packets were distributed to owners of damaged buildings. Inspection teams from the National Park Service were driven throughout the area by OPAT volunteers so that they could view stricken National Register properties. Their inspection reports were then circulated to owners and city agencies.

The preservation response in Oakland was indeed a team effort that saw us through those hectic, tension-filled days.

Annalee Allen
President, Oakland Heritage Alliance
Cochair, Oakland Preservation Assistance Team

ruption. Local libraries may be able to help with conservation efforts for books and similar collections involving documents.

State. At the state level, each governor's office has established, with federal assistance, a state emergency office under a director who reports directly to the governor. While these offices coordinate the distribution of state aid, one of their most important functions is acting as the eyes and ears of the federal government, where the bulk of emergency funding originates. State historic preservation offices took active roles in the 1989 disasters and are developing even greater emergency planning activities.

Federal. The federal government plays an important role in responding to disasters in the United States. For owners and managers of historic places, these basic disaster programs likely are too bureaucratic and cumbersome for immediate relief efforts. However, they are, in the long term, likely to be the main avenue for financial assistance after a serious disaster. When such an emergency strikes, preservationists and government planners both need to focus in two directions at the same time: on immediate relief activities as well as on putting in motion the machinery to coordinate long-term recovery efforts with the federal government.

As the Federal Emergency Management Agency says in its publication *A Guide to Federal Aid in Disasters*, "When disaster strikes or threatens, responsibility for protection, relief and recovery resides with the individuals and institutions affected, aided by State and local government and volunteer organizations. Under certain circumstances, however, when those resources are not enough, help from the Federal Government can be sought and provided. The President's Disaster Relief Program, managed by the Federal Emergency Management Agency, is the primary means of Federal aid—but not the only one."

For practical purposes, federal aid for disaster relief comes from two primary sources, FEMA and the Small Business Administration, and is financial in nature. Both FEMA and SBA operate like insurers of last resort, paying for damages above and beyond those covered by private insurance. With FEMA, assistance takes the form of grants to local governments and nonprofit organizations; with SBA, loans. FEMA in particular heavily emphasizes restoring the functions of government. Both programs are discussed in the chapter After a Disaster.

THE PRIVATE SECTOR

In the private sector, aid can be tapped in a variety of places—from local and state preservation groups to historic sites, from national associations and their members to individuals, paid and volunteer.

Emergency Stabilization in Charleston

As Hugo—a storm of unusual magnitude—approached, preservationists in Charleston discovered that we were without a cultural resource disaster preparedness plan. Cultural organizations were able only to perform basic protective measures for their museum properties.

After the storm Mayor Joseph P. Riley, Jr., called officials of the Historic Charleston Foundation to his office and asked us, along with the city preservation officer, to rally the preservation community and organize an emergency preservation stabilization service in the foundation's preservation center. With a phone bank and restored power, we began acting for the city, undertaking such tasks as registering arriving contractors in a special database and disseminating this information to owners of damaged historic buildings. We had the help of many—the Preservation Society of Charleston, National Trust, National Park Service, SHPOs, private consultants, architects, professors, students and National Roofing Contractors Association, among others.

Hugo taught us that a multilevel program of surveys, technical information, contractor database, fund raising and similar activities is crucial to build accurate data with which to assess the effects of a disaster and assist in the recovery, especially to ensure that preservation regulations are not compromised. Our new recording program with HABS and damage mitigation studies, being conducted with the aid of The Citadel and Cornell University, will help in any future catastrophe.

We strongly recommend having disaster plans and making sure that documentation on historic buildings is adequate, up-to-date and readily at hand.

Lawrence Walker, Executive Director
Historic Charleston Foundation

Organizations. Key players are local preservation groups, city and county historical societies, and area historic sites and museums. On the state level, statewide preservation groups and state historical societies also should be involved.

Professionals. Some of the most immediately usable help will come from those who know best: fellow preservationists. Professionals qualified to advise and work on historic structures, landscapes and collections should be identified in the planning process. Suggestions about organizations and professions in which to find them are given in Where to Get Help as well as in the chapter Before Disaster Strikes.

Volunteers. As the disasters of 1989 proved, many people want to help in an emergency. Ways should be developed to channel the energies of well-meaning volunteers. Charleston preservationists found that it was difficult to rely on in-town volunteers, because they had storm-related problems of their own; and that it was difficult to put some out-of-towners to work productively because of a mismatch of skills and needs. Volunteers may want to do what they want, rather than what the situation calls for. It is thus necessary to develop a system for directing volunteers in a disaster's aftermath, such as:

1 Clarify expectations on each side.

2 Define jobs to be done.

3 Set specific goals, weighing costs and benefits.

4 Persuade volunteers to do needed work that they may not have envisioned, such as answering telephones.

5 Provide recognition for volunteers' contributions, from public thanks to free lunches if the budget permits.

6 Say no to volunteers if you cannot adequately direct them.

Inventorying and Recording Losses and Damages

After any natural disaster, historic places will be in a wide range of conditions, from intact and unscathed, to in need of minor repair, to extensively damaged and, in some cases, to completely destroyed. Lost and damaged sites should be inventoried immediately as a prelude to preparing a more detailed record of specific damages. Documenting what happened allows preservationists and planners to understand the chain of events unleashed by natural forces, prepare a recovery plan, review and update emergency plans and stockpiled supplies, and try to mitigate future losses.

Inventorying losses uncovers a variety of aftereffects:

Total destruction. Historic buildings along an earthquake fault line may have crumpled to the ground. Houses may have been completely blown away by a hurricane or tornado. Fire may have obliterated a site and its collection. In such instances, quickly recording damages may be doubly important.

Obvious damage. In addition to total loss, other damage may also be obvious. As David Spell, proprietor of Charleston's Two Meeting Street Inn, told the *New York Times* after Hurricane Hugo, one stone-and-brick chimney was flung by the storm right through the inn's roof "and landed in a four-poster bed in a third-floor bedroom just like it was supposed to be there."

Hidden problems. Just as often, however, damage is hidden. Outside the hardest-hit areas in the San Francisco Bay Area, for example, the only clue to a serious shift in a structure's foundation often was a slightly out-of-level floor in one corner or damp soil near the foundation, evidence of failed water or sewer lines.

Serendipitous finds. The destruction additionally may reveal parts of structures or landscapes that are rarely open to inspection. At Drayton Hall, the National Trust property outside Charleston, Hugo's uprooting of trees unveiled several significant archeological sites, allowing previously impossible investigation into the early days of the plantation's daily life. Barclay Jones of Cornell University also reports that when Henry Kissinger's office at the Center for International Affairs in the Harvard Semitic Museum was bombed by protesters in 1970, a damage search discovered long-lost cartons in the attic. They contained 28,000 photographic records, the largest collection of pictures showing the Middle East during the 19th century.

The inventory of losses should occur in two or three stages:

1 A preliminary visual investigation to identify destroyed and damaged properties as well as ones that survived with minor or no effects. This stage's key goal is to identify historic structures in need of rapid and thorough examination.

2 A detailed follow-up evaluation, performed on those places isolated during the preliminary phase.

3 A more thorough structural analysis, carried out by specially qualified engineers, if warranted, followed by any necessary stabilization measures.

PRELIMINARY DAMAGE ASSESSMENT

Clearly, the more survey work accomplished before a disaster, the less arduous the task of damage assessment. To obtain a general idea of how historic sites fared, a quick, areawide inspection should be made as soon as it is possible to venture outside; a windshield survey by car or fast evaluation on foot is a good method. Then a more detailed site-by-site inventory should be conducted, as follows:

1 Collect historic resource surveys, landmarks lists and maps of the affected areas.

2 Organize and instruct teams of searchers, preferably including a preservation architect, engineer or other experienced professional; provide members with damage assessment forms or develop another systematic recording method.

3 Divide the affected area — town, district, neighborhood, streets or individual sites — into sections to be inventoried by each team.

4 Physically examine sites within each territory for losses and damages, recording a full range of conditions as shown on the sample damage assessment form here. Photographs or sketches of damages are essential.

5 If feasible, take aerial photographs of widespread damage, especially to compare with any predisaster views.

6 Compile information and prepare to make detailed follow-up safety evaluations of sites identified as needing reexamination or stabilization.

The area may contain one or several historic buildings of special significance, and these structures, perhaps National Historic Landmarks or sites in or eligible for the National Register of Historic Places, may warrant priority attention by investigators. If they hold national as well as local significance, these sites may command the early attention of expert teams from outside the region. For example, the Charleston hurricane assistance team dispatched by the National Park Service directed its survey efforts toward the 144 most significant structures in the two historic districts of the city, those judged "exceptional" in Charleston's 1975 architectural survey.

Following both the 1989 hurricane and earthquake, the Park Service's Historic American Buildings Survey also sent individuals to photograph damaged historic buildings. The most threatened structures were photographed so that an official record of them would exist in the event of their demolition; in California, in fact, many of those recorded were soon torn down. By using photogrammetric processes, measured photographs of unstable buildings were made without the team having to measure them by hand, as is usually required. The result is a record of buildings destroyed by Loma Prieta — preservation at least on paper.

RECORDING DAMAGES

Recording damages does not have to be a complicated or unnecessarily time-consuming process. The simpler the recording procedure, the more likely volunteers can be recruited and trained to do it accurately. The damage assessment form on the following pages can be used as a model:

Damage Assessment Form

Building Name _____

Address _____

City (or Vicinity) and County _____

Owner _____

Date of Construction _____ Tax Map No. _____

Primary Use
☐ Residential (1–2 units) ☐ Residential (3+ units) ☐ Office Building ☐ School
☐ Commercial ☐ Mixed ☐ Church ☐ Lodge
☐ Industrial/Warehouse ☐ Hotel/Motel ☐ Bank ☐ Other _____

Description
☐ Freestanding ☐ Row No. of Stories _____
☐ Basement ☐ Attic No. Chimney(s) _____

Construction Type
☐ Masonry Bearing Wall ☐ Veneer/Steel Frame ☐ Wood Frame ☐ Concrete
☐ Veneer/Concrete Frame ☐ Concrete Unit ☐ Other _____

Surface Covering
☐ Brick ☐ Stucco ☐ Wood Siding
☐ Stone ☐ Other _____ ☐ Roof _____

Foundation
☐ Concrete Slab ☐ Block ☐ Stone/Rubble ☐ Other _____ ☐ Unknown

Geological Nature of Site
☐ Bedrock ☐ Soil/Sand ☐ Fill ☐ Other _____ ☐ Unknown

Historical Designation
☐ National Register ☐ National Register District ☐ State ☐ Local
Survey Rating _____ ☐ None ☐ Unknown

Falling Hazards

	Hazard	No Apparent Hazard	Unknown	Comments
Parapet/Cornice	☐	☐	☐	_____
Ornamentation	☐	☐	☐	_____
Chimney(s)	☐	☐	☐	_____
Floors	☐	☐	☐	_____
Roof Structure	☐	☐	☐	_____
Equipment	☐	☐	☐	_____
Trees	☐	☐	☐	_____
Other	☐	☐	☐	_____

Damage Observations

Comments

Exterior Walls	_____	_____
Frame (General Condition)	_____	_____
Frame Members	_____	_____
Frame Connections	_____	_____
Roof Framing	_____	_____
Roof Covering	_____	_____
Chimney(s)	_____	_____
Doors	_____	_____
Windows and Shutters	_____	_____
Porch	_____	_____
Downspouts and Gutters	_____	_____
Interior Bearing/Shear Walls	_____	_____
Partitions (Nonbearing)	_____	_____
Floor(s)	_____	_____
Stair(s)	_____	_____
Glass	_____	_____
Mechanical Equipment	_____	_____
Electrical Equipment	_____	_____
Garden and Trees	_____	_____
Fences and Garden Walls	_____	_____
Walkways and Sidewalks	_____	_____
Other: _____	_____	_____
Total Damage	_____	_____

Overall Assessment

☐ No Damage or Easily Repairable
☐ Damage Repairable
☐ Damage Will Require Massive Repair/Reconstruction

Recommendations for Further Inspection _____

_____

Recommendations for Immediate Actions _____

_____

Recommendations for Future Repair Work _____

_____

Inspector(s) _____ **Agency** _____ **Date** _____

Photographs or Video (Roll and Numbers) _____

National Park Service Experts

At the request of local officials, the National Park Service organized teams of professionals to provide assistance following both Hurricane Hugo and the Loma Prieta earthquake.

For six weeks after Hugo, the Park Service rotated 13 professionals through Charleston on one- or two-week tours, eventually providing assessments of approximately 150 damaged buildings, giving technical aid to more than 1,000 owners and recording many damaged historic properties. Similarly, with help from the California state historic preservation office, after the earthquake a team of eight historic-architecture professionals prepared assessments of 90 buildings in Aptos, Gilroy, Hollister, Los Gatos, Oakland, Salinas, Santa Cruz, Watsonville and San Francisco.

Although these teams were very successful, the Park Service generally has not been able to provide this kind of assistance because of a lack of funding. But, based on the experience gained with these disasters, we can improve our effectiveness in future emergencies through better coordination with the Federal Emergency Management Agency; development of a national clearinghouse of experts in architectural conservation who are willing to be involved in disaster relief efforts; formation of several specialized core relief teams available for critical emergency assistance; and liaison with the SHPOs, National Trust, and professional and industrial groups to further support these activities. If additional funding were available, the Park Service also would prepare written guidelines and technical information to assist city officials and property owners and offer training courses for federal, state and local officials as well as private individuals likely to be involved in relief efforts.

Jerry L. Rogers
Associate Director, Cultural Resources, National Park Service

The preceding checklist synthesizes damage assessment forms used by National Park Service staff and local organizations after Hurricane Hugo and the Loma Prieta earthquake. Designed to fit on the front and back of one page, the form describes basic damages, some of which can be noted by volunteers; other questions, such as those relating to structural damage more typical of an earthquake, require specialized architectural or engineering knowledge. The form is suitable for rapid conversion and entry into a computerized database and can be used to provide the damage statistics needed for disaster relief. This form does not, however, provide data on collections or other assets inside a building.

When summarized, the information obtained with such forms can be used to draw up a recovery plan. The numbers allow projections of the amounts and kinds of supplies needed, setting of priorities for the work schedule, estimation of the types and hours of skilled workers needed, and direct the attention of local and outside experts to where they are needed most.

FOLLOW-UP SAFETY EVALUATION

After the Loma Prieta earthquake, building officials in California followed a three- or four-tier seismic-inspection procedure:

Classification	Color Tag	Description
Inspected	Green	No apparent hazard, but repairs may be required. Lateral load capacity not significantly decreased. No restriction on use or occupancy.
Limited Entry	Yellow	Dangerous condition believed to be present. Owner entry permitted only for emergency purposes and at own risk. No continuous use. Public entry not permitted. Possible aftershock hazard.
Unsafe	Red	Extreme hazard; may collapse, especially in an aftershock. Unsafe for occupancy or entry, except by authorities.
Potentially Unsafe	Pink	Potentially extreme hazard; may collapse. Danger of collapse from an aftershock. Unsafe for occupancy or entry, except by authorities or owner or tenant and an engineer for inspection.

Responding to the massive needs generated by Hugo and Loma Prieta, state historic preservation offices in affected areas such as South Carolina and California quickly realized that preservation programs were not well prepared to deal with disasters. They are planning for the next emergencies by assisting gubernatorial and legislative task forces, helping develop coordinated action plans for state agencies by:

1 Assigning distinct response roles as well as responsibilities for environmental and preservation review

2 Clarifying eligibility rules for aid from federal and state agencies to ensure that they are clear and consistently interpreted for historic properties

3 Preparing SHPOs to take the lead in coordinating preservation assistance from national and state sources

4 Reviewing other state agency plans that may allow preemptive actions harmful to historic properties, such as removing architectural details

5 Readying public service announcements that advise on key preservation actions and counsel against hasty moves that may cause harm

6 Supporting strong local preservation ordinances and education efforts, including review of how local building codes will be applied in a crisis

7 Encouraging a federal discretionary fund from which to make emergency grants for disaster recovery

8 Reviewing disaster-prone areas to determine whether additional inventory and planning efforts are needed by SHPOs

To prepare for an atmosphere characterized by chaos, panic and enormous pressures to reach rapid public safety decisions, SHPOs are paving the way for consideration of alternatives—the hallmark of preservation practice.

Eric Hertfelder, Executive Director
National Conference of State Historic Preservation Officers

DURING A DISASTER

This color-coded inspection procedure was recommended in two handbooks prepared by the Applied Technology Council of Redwood City, *Procedures for Postearthquake Safety Evaluation of Buildings* and *Field Manual: Postearthquake Safety Evaluation of Buildings.* As part of the first step—rapid, visual evaluation—a brief report is prepared, then buildings are tagged and placed into one of three categories, green, yellow or red, based on their perceived safety in their current state.

Yellow tags. One of the key purposes of this classification system is to single out buildings needing a more thorough examination. A second inspection, or detailed evaluation, is given only to buildings posted with yellow, or limited entry, tags. The detailed evaluation is carried out a few hours or days after the preliminary observation. According to the manual, it "should be performed by a structural engineer (or geotechnical specialist if this discipline is required), preferably as a member of a team of at least two persons. They are to make a detailed visual examination of the questionable structure for purposes of assessing whether the building is (1) apparently safe and can be used, even though it may require repairs; (2) unsafe, and must not be entered by anyone; or (3) still questionable and must be subject to an engineering evaluation."

Red tags. The third tier, or engineering evaluation, is also quite specific: it should be done only "after a visual examination by one or more structural engineers has been made without having resolved the safety of the building. This procedure...may require anywhere from a few days to a week or more to complete" and may require removal of portions of the building and possible destructive testing and structural calculations.

The red tag was designed as a convenience for investigators, meaning only that the preliminary examination had found obvious, but not necessarily fatal, damages to a structure. On the other hand, red tags accomplished the first goal: keeping people out until a more detailed examination could take place.

Seeing red. After Loma Prieta, many buildings throughout northern California were inspected and then posted with red tags. But without explanation of what red-tagging meant, many persons in the public and the media concluded that the structures were condemned and subject to immediate demolition. The situation became so serious that National Trust Advisor Bruce D. Judd, AIA, issued a special flyer noting that none of the categories says anything about demolition and addressing the erroneous presumption "that this demolition must happen immediately."

The classifications outlined here do not address the future of historic buildings that, even though damaged by disaster, may be stabilized, restored and used again. From this insight came the "second opinion" campaign, discussed next.

Protecting Historic Resources After a Disaster

In the rush to "get back to normal" after a disaster, unthinking or seemingly uncontrollable actions may hurt historic resources:

1 Restorable buildings are torn down.

2 Architectural elements are carted away with the debris.

3 Trees are tossed out rather than replanted.

4 Property owners make hasty and inappropriate repairs.

5 Archeological resources are disturbed by heavy equipment.

6 Government agencies — such as building permit offices and landmarks commissions — may operate with conflicting goals.

7 Normal design review procedures for changes to historic properties may be suspended.

8 A crush of construction applications may overburden officials.

9 Inspections of historic structures may be carried out by persons with minimal or no qualifications, including volunteer structural engineers and other experts from outside the area.

As Jerry Rogers, associate director for cultural resources of the National Park Service, said after Hurricane Hugo, "Sometimes disaster relief is as bad as the disaster. Very few people have the power of those in charge of cleanup."

Protecting historic places and artifacts in the immediate aftermath of a disaster involves answering several related questions. The first, in the immediate aftermath, is, What must be done to avoid further damage through inappropriate public and private actions? Next, How can the potential for rehabilitation be assessed? What technical and financial incentives can be offered to help make rehabilitation feasible and attractive? And then, as long-term recovery begins, How can historic property review processes be adhered to despite the emergency conditions?

The answers are the same as during normal times: vigilantly monitoring official actions; surveying the condition of historic properties; providing grants for professional assistance as well as low-interest stabilization loans; conducting public education; and carrying out vigorous political advocacy.

Fortunately, there are strong arguments in favor of preservation, not the least of which is the continuity of the community. Stabilizing and retrofitting historic structures to meet code standards also may be more cost effective than replacing them. Commercial property owners, in particular, may find that demolition for new construction causes them to lose the competitive edge that only a historic building can provide.

GETTING A "SECOND OPINION"

About a month after the 1989 earthquake, Mark P. Ryser, executive director of the Foundation for San Francisco's Architectural Heritage, wrote to his members: "Decisions critical to the preservation of San Francisco's architectural legacy are being made by engineers and inspectors, many of whom have little interest in or understanding of older buildings." With this concern in mind, California preservationists launched a campaign asking that building owners and government officials get a "second opinion" before taking the precipitate action of demolishing historic structures.

Just as in medicine, advocates for old buildings believed that taking a careful, disinterested look at damaged historic places might reveal a rehabilitation strategy involving only "minor surgery." "It's essential to get cities to slow down a bit and take a closer look," California Deputy State Historic Preservation Officer Steade Craigo said at the time. "There was a real panic in these areas and there was a lot of red-tagging."

In retrospect, this campaign had significant results. While building inspections in San Francisco began the day after the quake, it soon became apparent that serious flaws existed in coordinating the inventory process. Inspectors often reevaluated and changed the status of historic structures, even on a daily basis. Moreover, even the incomplete compilations of damaged sites were not easily cross-referenced with rosters of city landmarks. This made getting a "second opinion" much more difficult — and at the same time more necessary.

A similar scenario was played out in Santa Cruz, which became a focus of the "do something now" response to earthquake damage. Appearing before the city council, Kathryn Burns, director of the National Trust's Western Regional Office, advised that "unless a damaged building poses a clear and imminent physical danger to lives or other property, which cannot be avoided by means less drastic than demolition, the city would be on tenuous legal ground if it summarily ordered a demolition without opportunity for review by the owner, the historic preservation commission and the public."

Burns's prescription was bolstered by California law but is a review procedure that is not altogether different from recommended preservation practice. Her suggestions provide a model process for other communities and other types of disasters:

DEMOLITION REVIEW PROCEDURES

1 Any building proposed for demolition by either its owner or the city building or fire officials should be examined by a structural engineer qualified to assess the building's potential for rehabilitation in place, dismantling or other measures that would mitigate total demolition. Only then can it be determined that demolition is necessary to remove an unsafe condition.

2 Decisions on demolition must result from interdisciplinary evaluations and community consensus. For example, not only is a structural engineer's outside opinion required, the preservation commission's evaluation also should be sought and considered.

3 In proposing a particular action, alternatives must also be presented, together with an explanation of why they are considered unacceptable. If rehabilitation is considered unacceptable, clearly defined costs or other reasons must be set forth.

4 The public should be given a reasonable opportunity to review and comment on the recommendations of city officials before a final decision is made on demolition.

5 Any decisions must consider the cumulative impact of all proposed demolitions. Decisions on specific buildings should be withheld until a decision is made affecting the entire area.

6 Because the ultimate decision on whether or not to demolish a building still standing inherently calls for political judgment—that is, whether the social costs of preservation outweigh the social costs of demolition—that decision must be reviewed and accepted by elected officials before it is allowed to take effect.

LEGISLATION

In addition to ensuring that existing regulations are followed, special legislation or legislative resolutions can underscore the importance of protecting historic places. Public Resources Code 5028, passed by the California legislature in an emergency session following the Loma Prieta earthquake, requires that any building "listed on the National Register, on the California Register of Historic Places, or on any local public register of historic places, and that has been damaged due to a natural disaster, including...an earthquake... may (not) be demolished, destroyed or significantly altered, except for restoration to preserve or enhance its historical values, unless the structure presents an imminent threat to the public of bodily harm or of damage to adjacent property, or unless the State Historic Preservation Office determines...that the structure may be demolished, destroyed or significantly altered." The National Trust, in a bulletin about emergency financial assistance programs one month after the quake, noted that any demolition proposed at that late date under an immediate-danger exception "may be unjustified and is certainly questionable."

Stabilizing Damaged Sites

After concerns for human safety are satisfied, practical steps must be taken to shore up structures and keep out the elements so that they do no further harm to historic buildings and collections. It is worthwhile to recall that major damage after Hurricane Hugo's rampage—in fact, a significant portion of total damages—came when torrential rains fell through breached roofs and windows just a few days after the hurricane had passed through. In earthquake zones it is good to remember that a strong temblor typically will be followed by thousands of aftershocks, even three to six months after the quake; these ground shakings can pose particular hazards to people involved in repairing damaged buildings.

EMERGENCY STABILIZATION

Basic steps. Stabilization steps will, in large part, be basic manual labor: installing temporary window and door coverings of plastic and plywood; covering damaged roofs; shoring up damaged walls; removing dangerous limbs from injured trees; covering and protecting valuable objects exposed to weather; and identifying and clearly marking objects that should not be disturbed or should be salvaged during general cleanup. Particular care should be taken that the materials used for stabilization are not in themselves of historical value, for example, timbers and beams used for bracing walls as well as bricks used to fill holes. This rule, however, should be broken when inaction may lead to further, often greater, damage.

Moisture. Regardless of the nature of the disaster, among the most important stabilization measures to take for historic structures are those that reduce threats brought by water. The National Park Service prepared the following moisture-reduction recommendations for the Historic Charleston Foundation after Hurricane Hugo:

1 Open your windows. Natural ventilation is preferable to mechanical dehumidification, which may cause damage to some building materials.

2 Remove standing water. Water left in basements will slowly evaporate and saturate masonry, wood and plaster.

3 Remove water-logged debris from basements and other areas that may be holding water.

4 Check plumbing for leaks.

5 Maintain protective roof coverings. Continued attention must be paid to temporary repairs. Repairing gutters and downspouts will help move water away from the building.

6 Provide reasonable heating when conditions allow but do not rush. Natural drying is preferable to heat.

7 Check plaster for looseness. Refasten with screw buttons where needed.

8 Remove moisture in a gradual and controlled process. Do not be in too big a hurry. Radical moisture changes may be more harmful than the moisture itself.

9 Watch for mildew as an indicator of high moisture levels.

Repair and demolition permits. Be aware that regulations govern even temporary repairs to structures. Almost all local governments will require permits for this kind of work, just as they would in normal times, to make sure that, first, structural integrity investigations have been carried out and, second, that emergency work will not further endanger life or property. Usually, an expedited process will be set up for work considered to be "repairs." Needless to say, demolitions are not "repairs," and they require demolition permits; preservationists should pay close attention to what is happening to historic structures in the field, as well as in the permit-issuing offices. They should insist that rigorous controls be placed on demolition activities. Having an established relationship that predates a disaster makes cooperation easier afterward. Even if permitting procedures are relaxed, preservationists can distribute information on correct rehabilitation techniques.

SECURITY CONSIDERATIONS

An essential corollary to stabilization immediately after a natural disaster is security. Because just as wind and rain can infiltrate, or inundate, through violated roofs and windows, valuable objects can as easily be carted away, whether by looters or in the course of improperly supervised rescue and relief operations. Time is of the essence in establishing security.

The potential damage caused by relief operations themselves cannot be underestimated. As Connie Wyrick of the Historic Charleston Foundation told the *New York Times* shortly after Hurricane Hugo passed: "Our biggest problem and greatest fear is that architectural elements, the cornices, the facings, are in the gutters and among curbside debris. We're just horrified that some of this might be carried away in the cleanup."

Remember also that security systems in daily use during normal times may have been rendered inoperable. For public sites, from the largest historic site complex to the smallest house museum, at least one authorized staff member must be on site. Larger organizations with full-time security staff should activate disaster contingency plans immediately.

Further problems arise with collections, especially books and documents. The Northeast Document Conservation Center in Massachusetts advises giving high priority to salvaging the catalog and other records of a collection. In fact, where there is only minimal warning that a disaster is about to strike, all library disaster preparedness plans advise waterproofing the catalog first. The center recommends that "salvage operations should avoid any action that might remove or deface identifying marks and labels. When part or all of the catalog or bibliographic records have been lost, it may be necessary to make a chart of the flooded area and label each item as it is withdrawn to show its location.... One or more persons must be assigned specific responsibility for making such records because the time and expense involved in subsequent identification and recataloging of damaged materials can be substantial."

The center endorses the following first-response salvage procedures for collections:

1 In winter, turn off all heat in the building. In summer, reduce the temperature as much as possible through air conditioning, if available. (If freezing temperatures are expected, take into account the possibility of frozen pipes bursting, adding to water damages.)

2 Create maximum air flow through all affected areas by opening doors and windows. If electrical facilities are operational, use as many fans as you can acquire to create a current of air directed to expel humid air from the building. If dehumidifiers are available they may be used with fans for small enclosed areas. The objective is to avoid pockets of stagnant, moist air.

3 If electricity is not available, hire portable generators to power lights, fans, dehumidifiers and other electrical services. For safety, all electrical lines should be waterproofed and grounded.

4 Do not permit anyone to open wet books, separate single sheets, remove covers when materials are water soaked or disturb wet file boxes, prints, drawings and photographs. Such handling can result in extensive and often irreparable damage to materials that otherwise might be salvaged. Reducing the cost of future restoration must be one of the top priorities of the salvage operation.

5 Organize a disaster response team and prepare a comprehensive plan of action, as well as plans for different contingencies.

6 Do not remove materials from the area until an overall plan with a schedule of priorities has been established and all personnel thoroughly briefed.

7 Canvass the community to locate freezing and storage space.

8 Seek the advice of specialists who can assist at the site of the disaster.

Manuscripts and single-sheet materials are specially troublesome when they are scattered by wind, water or shaking. Photographs of the disaster scene before salvage, or even a crude diagram, can be helpful in recovery efforts.

Communicating in an Emergency

In the immediate aftermath of the Loma Prieta earthquake, the "second opinion" campaign was a master stroke of public relations. It is a phrase that everybody understands, short enough that when uttered during a television "sound bite" still leaves time for the person interviewed to make an additional point about a threatened historic structure. When newspaper reporters use the phrase, "second opinion" will almost always appear within quotation marks, further driving home to the public the basic idea: slow down and take time to carefully consider the situation before taking irreversible action.

Across the country, following Hurricane Hugo, Charleston preservationists were faced with a similarly urgent public relations problem: how to urge people who wanted to rebuild immediately to take stock and then, at an appropriate time, take the right rehabilitation steps. Communicating was a challenge when the normal communications systems — mail, telephones — were out of order. The Preservation Society of Charleston quickly produced a flyer telling property owners, for example, to opt just for temporary roofing and to delay getting permanent replacement parts for their historic buildings until the proper materials and help could be obtained. This advice was conveyed also by word of mouth at first, then through seminars. The goal was to educate property owners, then contractors and insurance adjusters. "It was important," said Executive Director John Meffert, "that our publications looked good as well. Good-looking materials could be trusted to have good advice."

Keeping the lines of communication open, both during an emergency and immediately afterward, is an important part of the planning process.

THE FIRST HOURS

Mystic Seaport's emergency manual, outlined on pages 104–05, includes a subplan for the public affairs department that anticipates inquiries from the media and the public. It directs that these inquiries and the dissemination of news be coordinated and in most cases, handled by the department. It includes office and home telephone numbers for public affairs staff, together with the following emergency procedures:

Condition Watch (storm possible within 48 hours)

1 The public affairs director will be advised by the director, deputy director or, if necessary, other senior staff when an emergency is anticipated. He will, in turn, advise the public affairs staff.

2 In the event Condition Watch is established when the Seaport is closed, the department may require one staff member to be on the premises during evening hours.

3 Public affairs will establish and maintain contact with the central control station and compile and update information regularly.

4 Public affairs will answer public and media inquiries as appropriate.

5 Telephone switchboard will be provided with information as appropriate.

6 The department will be aware of docking situation and communicate information as appropriate.

Condition I (storm expected in 36 hours)

1 Condition Watch procedures are intensified.

2 Department staff will remove electric typewriters and other valuable equipment to second floor of Greenman House, or to other secure area depending on circumstances at the time. Other long lead-time preparations carried out.

3 Travel development will contact appropriate motorcoach companies to alert them of storm in area and possible museum closing.

4 Museum remains open to visitors during this period.

5 Dock master closes docks to arriving yachtsmen, requests departure of visiting yachts.

6 Depending on conditions, staff members may be available to assist other departments. Public affairs director will keep central control station informed as to staff availability for reassignment.

Condition II (destructive winds and high tides expected in 12 to 18 hours)

1 Designated staff members will report to the office.

2 Contact will be maintained with central control station.

3 A communications center will be established from public affairs office and central control station. Information will be updated regularly.

4 Public affairs will answer media inquiries and advise local press of conditions and future plans. Information will be provided on any Seaport closing plans.

DURING A DISASTER

5 No press admitted to grounds without accompanying public affairs staff.

Condition III (storm imminent)

1 All preventive measures should have been taken. Security force and other essential staff stand by. Others relieved of duties.

2 Museum closed to public.

Poststorm

1 Designated staff members report for duty.

2 Public affairs will maintain contact with central control for information on damage, cleanup and reopening. Information will be disseminated to the press and public as appropriate.

3 Equipment and department materials will be returned to proper places.

4 When motorcoach groups caught in the storm show up unexpectedly immediately after reopening and ask for assistance, travel development will handle as appropriate.

Emergency Seaport Media Contact

In the unlikely event that no member of the public affairs department is available to perform the necessary press liaison responsibility, the senior staff member on duty should assign another person. All press information should be given out by this one person to avoid conflicting statements and incorrect information being issued. It is the Seaport's policy to be helpful and truthful with reporters, and to treat all print and broadcast reporters equally and without favoritism.

THE AFTERMATH

During a natural disaster, newspapers and the broadcast media may not be in operation. But in the aftermath they will be among the first institutions to resume full operations, even before the widespread resumption of electrical and telephone service. This is when the one person designated to handle communications responsibilities for historic sites or preservation teams can play a significant role, especially if good relations have been established with key media personalities beforehand. This person should be prepared to mount a prompt outreach campaign to the public, through the media, with accurate information about damages, recovery plans and correct preservation procedures.

Sample materials include the following:

News kit or press release. A kit that makes the public and public officials aware of the needs of a historic site, district or preservation generally does not have to be elaborate. At its most basic, a simple press release will suffice. It should include, at the top, the name and telephone number of the person to be contacted for more information.

News angle. Any communication with the media, even if its primary purpose is to describe what to do and not to do about historic objects and places, should begin with a news angle, or "hook." It should, in short, begin with a news release that reads like a news story, with the "who, what, where, when, why and how" information in the lead sentences. The lead may describe damages and cleanup progress. Or it may be an appeal for volunteer help. A photograph, if possible, with a short caption will add impact to the release.

Background information. With the hard news taken care of in the release, background information may be provided so that a reporter can fill out a story line — such as more general material on area damages and procedures for protecting historic structures and objects.

Op-ed feature. Another useful item, if time and circumstances permit, is an opinion feature prepared for a newspaper's op-ed page. This would be a "guest opinion" by the director of a preservation organization, agency or historic site. Such a piece should be in the range of 750 words typed double-spaced and written clearly and concisely. Op-ed articles should be submitted to the editorial page editor of newspapers or the editorial director of local television or radio stations. While broadcast outlets are not going to use a 750-word essay, the ideas presented may lead to a 10-, 30- or even 60-second story, feature or editorial.

It is also important to recognize that radio and television are the primary sources of news for more than three-quarters of the American people. And all press information must go to the right person at each newspaper or broadcast outlet, even if it means walking several miles and climbing over downed trees to do so.

AFTER A DISASTER

Recovery Procedures

Putting things "right" after a disaster
is an important part of the recovery process.
Charleston had many roofs to repair after Hugo,
including one that blew off
the Cathedral of St. Luke and St. Paul.
(Jack E. Boucher, HABS)

LOMA PRIETA flattened the double-

deck section of Interstate 880 that cut through downtown Oakland, Calif., killing 42 people. Construction of the highway in the 1950s split a neighborhood in two, a not-uncommon experience during the height of the freeway-building era. When the quake destroyed the freeway section at Cypress Street, neighborhood residents mourned the casualties but viewed the demise of the road as a great opportunity.

"When they first built the Cypress freeway, we were a minority black community that was totally controlled by a white power structure," Oakland community activist Bill Love told the "MacNeil/Lehrer NewsHour" a year after the quake. "Today, the mayor's black, our supervisor's black, our city council person's black, the majority of the city council's black, 30 percent of the board of supervisors is black, the speaker of the assembly is black. We now have people who will in fact listen to us."

Bill Love's aim is revitalization of his neighborhood. And the earthquake has galvanized many local residents like him into seeking that goal. On the first anniversary of the earthquake, community residents dedicated a living memorial of 42 cypress trees in the former freeway's right-of-way.

This same spirit of recovery echoed 3,000 miles away on the South Carolina coast after Hurricane Hugo, when local residents repeatedly told the *Washington Post*, "You should have seen it six months ago." Of course, as Meggett Lavin, curator of the National Trust's Drayton Hall, also said, "We start feeling good. And then a devotee comes in almost in tears, and the mourning process begins again. We try to perk them up."

Natural disasters cause irrevocable change. The only way to approach one's aftermath is to view it as an opportunity: to use the recovery process as an educational laboratory and to explore ways of making historic structures more resistant to the violent forces of nature, even to study new aspects of history revealed by the damage.

Scheduling Work: Repair in Haste, Repent at Leisure

The key word for ensuring that historic buildings recover from a disaster is patience. As John Meffert, executive director of the Preservation Society of Charleston, notes, "Repair in haste, repent at leisure."

In Charleston roofs in particular became a much-discussed topic, because so many of them were damaged — in many cases exposing roof substrates that went back to the colonial period. The destruction also quickly brought roofing contractors who flocked to Charleston from as far away as Chicago and Ireland, some of whom did work of the highest quality, others who did not. To protect consumers from unscrupulous contractors, the city consequently required all contractors working after the storm to be licensed and fingerprinted. Even then, some of the work was not acceptable.

The National Roofing Contractors Association sent a rotating disaster response team to the city to answer questions from homeowners about good roofing practice and to establish a clearinghouse for roofing information, in cooperation with the Historic Charleston Foundation. One of this team's inspection reports, involving a residence on the South Battery, illustrates the pitfalls of hasty repairs: "Contractor had previously been instructed on proper installation details for standing-seam metal. He has not followed recommendations. Panels are face-nailed and caulked. Edge details are poorly done. Black paint has been applied and dripped on side of house. Contractor claims that metal was etched with acid to receive paint; veracity is in doubt. Using half-round aluminum gutters with galvanized hangers pop-riveted into gutter. *Poor quality in general.*"

LONG-TERM RECOVERY SCHEDULE

Emphasizing patience, and realizing that recovering from a disaster will not take place overnight, a schedule for recovery activities can be developed. Needs will vary depending especially on the type of disaster faced. For example, areas affected by earthquakes may advise retrofitting and strengthening unreinforced masonry buildings where feasible. In its report on Hurricane Hugo, the National Trust recommended a recovery schedule for the affected areas that can be applied broadly to historic places after similar natural disasters:

IMMEDIATE TO ONE YEAR

Stabilization

1 Ensure that all damaged structures have adequate temporary covers and shoring.

Evaluation of damage to buildings is one of the first and most essential steps to undertake after a disaster. In the days following a severe hurricane or earthquake, building departments and private engineers work long hours; only they can say which damaged buildings are safe to enter. Hurricanes and earthquakes cause harm in different ways, so evaluation is different for each.

In a hurricane, damage comes from without, most commonly affecting a building's skin. Hurricanes commonly bring losses by flooding and wind that may carry flying debris, resulting in nonstructural damage. But severe structural damage also can occur; buildings have collapsed during major hurricanes.

In an earthquake, forces come from beneath the building and therefore affect the entire structure. The key difference in structural inspection is that a hurricane is a single event and an earthquake is not. Earthquake-damaged buildings must be inspected not just for damage but for their ability to withstand aftershocks as well.

This is where the risk to historic structures comes in. Communities want to get things back to normal, removing debris and clearing streets. The buildings that are not easy to fix may have a demolition order placed on them. It is easier to demolish than to undergo the far more difficult process of piecemeal repair. Public and official pressure to demolish may mean the loss of significant historic places. Understanding laws and policies for disaster relief is vital — or else historic structures may be bulldozed away.

Melvyn Green, Structural Engineer
Manhattan Beach, Calif.

2 Complete assessment of damaged public buildings.

3 Protect damaged buildings and sites from unauthorized borrowing of materials.

4 Complete documentation of sites and structures beyond salvage.

5 Stabilize damaged archeological sites.

6 Initiate organization of a preservation emergency response team.

7 Salvage representative pieces of buildings for documentation purposes.

8 Salvage building materials for possible reuse.

9 Begin to develop funding strategies.

Restoration

1 Start reforestation and replanting of significant streetscapes and landscapes.

2 Replace damaged and destroyed street furnishings.

Conservation

1 Begin monitoring environmental effects on damaged structures and landscapes.

2 Initiate field research on conservation needs of materials.

Protection

1 Start review and coordination of disaster agency compliance with federal historic preservation procedures and responsibilities.

2 Establish code review procedures to monitor proposed amendments.

Identification

1 Begin or complete full assessment of National Register of Historic Places resources.

2 Initiate survey and assessment of undocumented resources.

3 Complete assessment of threatened sites.

4 Begin documentation of damaged historic landscapes.

5 If damage is storm related, identify meteorological variables for correlation with structural research.

Education

1 Ensure the widest possible dissemination of current standard literature to owners, contractors and architects.

2 Provide technical consultation services to property owners.

3 Conduct seminars for disaster relief agencies on compliance with the Secretary of the Interior's Standards for Rehabilitation.

4 Conduct seminars for contractors.

5 Develop broad strategies for dealing with specific issues such as the potential loss of the wood building tradition.

6 Initiate examination of insurance issues, coverages and definitions.

7 Develop a workshop agenda for owners on specific topics such as tin roofing and decorative trim.

ONE TO THREE YEARS

Restoration

1 Begin restoration of buildings funded by grant programs.

Conservation

1 Establish a regional materials conservation laboratory to address specific needs.

Protection

1 Start preparation of preventive maintenance manuals for specific localities and building types.

2 Initiate a historic property owner's manual.

3 Expand protection of local historic districts.

4 Create new conservation districts including archeological sites.

5 Launch investigation of roof systems including structure, form, pitch, coverings and connectors to determine causes of failure and survival.

6 Investigate retrofitting programs for application to all endangered structures.

7 Initiate research into storm performance of shutters and window and door assemblies.

Identification

1 Initiate expanded survey and registration efforts in geographic and theme areas previously underrepresented, such as vernacular architecture, rural resources and cemeteries.

2 Ensure that sites and areas threatened by specific disaster types or vulnerable to development are surveyed.

Education

1 Prepare historic landscape rehabilitation guidelines.

2 Prepare infill design guidelines for communities.

3 Prepare specific area rehabilitation guidelines.

4 Initiate preservation crafts training programs in local or regional techniques and systems.

5 Broaden workshop programs and scope of publications as research is completed and reports are written.

THREE TO FIVE YEARS

Protection

1 Initiate planning and redesign studies for areas vulnerable to inappropriate redevelopment.

Identification

1 Expand the recording capabilities and accessibility of surveys.

2 Increase computerized records-management capabilities.

Education

1 Develop and test models of structural and retrofitting technology for historic buildings.

2 Implement demonstration projects.

Within this broad framework, the timing of disaster recovery will depend on the availability of money, labor and materials, both locally and nationally. Probably the most important ingredient in recovery will be the local political attitude toward and support for old buildings.

Maintaining Preservation Standards

Common effects of disasters on historic places—cracked walls, blown-off roofs, water-damaged plaster, wet furnishings and papers, and damaged trees—can usually be fixed. Although the aftermath of a disaster is not "preservation as usual," generally accepted standards should be followed even in the rush to repair.

BETTER TO REPAIR

For historic buildings, several general and broad rules-of-thumb are good guides after disasters, as well as before:

Repair rather than replace. Retain original features and materials wherever possible. Repair is historically and economically preferable to replacement.

Replace with similar features. If replacement is necessary, use items that match the originals in design and materials.

Retain historical character. If matching replacements are impossible because features are unavailable or too expensive, at least reproduce the salient visual characteristics of the original, such as material, composition, proportion and color.

Return to the original. Wherever possible, replace previously missing parts and remove inappropriate modernizations.

Recovery after a disaster may uncover some out-of-the-ordinary philosophical restoration issues. For example, if a historic roof failed because it was an improper design for a building, or improperly installed, must it be restored exactly as it was before the disaster? Concerns such as these should be taken up with a restoration architect or other qualified professional.

THE SECRETARY'S STANDARDS

The Secretary of the Interior's Standards for Rehabilitation, issued by the National Park Service, provide a valuable framework for planning disaster recovery procedures. They are usually applied to rehabilitation projects undertaken without the added stress of sudden damage to historic resources, but these standards should be kept in mind for all preservation work:

1 A property shall be used for its historic purpose or be placed in a new use that requires minimal change to the defining characteristics of the building and its site and environment.

2 The historic character of a property shall be retained and preserved. The removal of historic materials or alteration of features and spaces that characterize a property shall be avoided.

3 Each property shall be recognized as a physical record of its time, place and use. Changes that create a false sense of historical development, such as adding conjectural features or architectural elements from other buildings, shall not be undertaken.

4 Most properties change over time; those changes that have acquired historical significance in their own right shall be retained and preserved.

5 Distinctive features, finishes and construction techniques or examples of craftsmanship that characterize a historic property shall be preserved.

6 Deteriorated historic features shall be repaired rather than replaced. Where the severity of deterioration requires replacement of a distinctive feature, the new feature shall match the old in design, color, texture and other visual qualities and, where possible, materials. Replacement of missing features shall be substantiated by documentary, physical or pictorial evidence.

7 Chemical or physical treatments, such as sandblasting, that cause damage to historic materials shall not be used. The surface cleaning of structures, if appropriate, shall be undertaken using the gentlest means possible.

8 Significant archeological resources affected by a project shall be protected and preserved. If such resources must be disturbed, mitigation measures shall be undertaken.

9 New additions, exterior alterations or related new construction shall not destroy historic materials that characterize the property. The new work shall be differentiated from the old and shall be compatible with the massing, size, scale and architectural features to protect the historical integrity of the property and its environment.

10 New additions and adjacent or related new construction shall be undertaken in such a manner that, if removed in the future, the essential form and integrity of the historic property and its environment would be unimpaired.

The Interior Department guidelines note specifically that "repairs and alterations must not damage or destroy materials, features or finishes that are important in defining the building's historic character. For example, certain treatments—if improperly applied—may cause or accelerate physical deterioration of a historic building." Such actions include improper repointing or exterior masonry cleaning techniques, or use of insulation that damages the historic fabric. Sandblasting never meets these standards.

Rehabilitation After a Disaster

The photograph that graced the pages of the *San Juan Star* on October 2, 1989, was riveting. Dangling from an enormous construction crane—like a fish out of water on the end of a line—was a 100-foot tall, 134-year-old Banyan tree, toppled by Hurricane Hugo. But quick action, aided by three cranes and a steel-cable support system, allowed the historic tree to be placed upright once again in its customary spot near the pool at the El San Juan Hotel. While not typically so dramatic, the techniques of sensitive rehabilitation can bring disaster-damaged historic structures and landscapes back to life.

In general terms, rehabilitation proceeds on three tracks: exterior, interior and landscape. Work in these three areas can occur simultaneously, with the added caveat that roofs and walls must be secure and watertight, even on a temporary basis, and that some landscape features can be rescued if action is taken immediately after the damage happens. Much of the following advice was prepared by the National Park Service for the Historic Charleston Foundation to use in postdisaster rehabilitation.

ROOFS

Every historic structure has a roof, a built-up system finished with a waterproof layer exposed to the elements. It may be wood shingle or shake, standing-seam metal, slate or tile. It may be steeply pitched or nearly flat. But it will begin with a layer of sheathing, or substrate, and finish with an outer layer of covering material.

When the substrate that holds the waterproof layer deteriorates, as through excessive moisture in an attic caused by inadequate ventilation, the fasteners that hold the outer covering may lose their grip. All might be well with such a roof on a bright, sunny day, even during a thunderstorm, but not when hurricane or tornado winds begin to blow.

1 Because a roof is damaged does not mean that it is a complete loss. Get expert advice, particularly because damage may not be visible.

2 Metal roofing may be more difficult to repair, especially when wind damage has bent it out of shape. Portions, however, may be reusable.

3 Metal flashings, at chimneys, dormers, valleys, ridges and porches, are especially vulnerable and should be thoroughly checked.

4 Gutters and downspouts should function properly. In most cases, having no gutters and downspouts is preferable to damaged ones, which may channel water directly into a building.

5 Metal types should not be mixed. Incompatible fasteners, for example, may quickly corrode under normal weather conditions, leaving the roof unattached for all practical purposes.

6 Tar is a handy and speedy temporary repair material. But do not rely on it in any quantity, because it probably will have to be removed when permanent repairs are made.

Under the roof. Roofs may also cover a hidden account of a historic structure's past. Just as uprooted trees sometimes reveal archeologically significant sites, roofs tend to preserve a chronological record of change. Rows of nails may indicate the earlier existence of a roof, or a series of roofs may have been laid one on top of the other, with the original covering at the bottom. These discoveries may be important finds — even if not evidence of good roofing practice.

Postdisaster education. Charleston is a city of slate roofs, a fact that permitted much post-Hugo attention to focus on this specific rehabilitation problem. A coalition of local preservation organizations held a series of seminars, open to the public, on various technical topics, including roofing. The sessions covered the requirements of the city's architectural review board, providing tips about negotiating with insurance adjusters and the Federal Emergency Management Agency. And they provided building owners the opportunity to ask hard questions of experts from the preservation, roofing, insurance and legal professions.

Following are pointers developed to help property owners repair damaged slate roofs:

1 Weatherize your home by drying it with temporary roofing material, from a minimum of 43-pound felt to 90-pound roll roofing.

2 Provide a complete slate sample to the Historic Charleston Foundation for color and size matching, or you may rely on a qualified roofing contractor to do this for you. All samples should have a label securely attached to them indicating the name of the homeowner, the address, the approximate age of the structure and a telephone number. If your roof has a variety of sizes and colors be sure to supply several representative examples.

3 Select a roofing contractor with the following qualifications:
Previous slate application experience
A current license issued by the city of Charleston
Adequate proof of workers compensation and liability insurance
A minimum of three references for similar jobs completed within the last six
    months
A list of principal suppliers that can be called for credit references
Membership in local roofing trade associations

4 Have your contractor determine how much slate is required. Be sure that your contractor determines whether or not any of the existing slate on the roof can be reused or salvaged. Obtain a written estimate of the cost to repair or replace the roof, which should include disposal of old roofing material and cleanup cost.

5 Contact your insurance agent with an estimate of the cost and steps you have taken to weatherize your home. Secure written approval of the estimate provided.

6 Obtain architectural review board approval if there is a change in the size or color of slate.

7 Review cost estimates and let the contract.

MASONRY

Masonry walls (brick or stone held together with mortar) may either fail completely in an earthquake or storm, especially if its roof is lifted off, allowing winds to hit the walls, or to succumb to water damage. Another immediate victim is chimneys. The most common long-term problem is cracking and settling, followed by mortar deterioration.

Foundations. Cracking and settling will probably show up first in foundations. Typical problems of masonry foundations are, first, failure because of soil settlement. When the soil characteristics around and under a structure allow it to settle unevenly — whether because of catastrophic rainfall, downspout or gutter failure, improper grading, infiltrating tree roots or, most likely, a combination of these factors — the underpinnings of a historic building may simply wash away.

Historic buildings tended to be built with improper footings, unless they were anchored in stone. Until the turn of the 20th century, most if not all foundations were dug by hand. Even in recent years in earthquake zones the extent of a foundation may be a poured concrete slab, the perfect platform from which to transmit lateral vibrations through a masonry structure. When foundations fail, a professional engineer must be consulted, but nonstructural cracks may be easier to repair.

Mortar. The second set of problems arise through the deterioration of mortar joints, which can be encouraged by hurricane and tornado winds and earthquake shaking. Settlement from either cause leads to cracking in masonry walls and compromise of the structure. The National Park Service advises that:

1 Compatibility of materials is important. Similar brick types should be used in repairs. Portland cement mortar or stucco should be avoided.

2 A good type of mortar to use for most brick is one composed of lime, sand and some portland cement. A typical mix might include three parts lime, one part portland cement and 10 to 12 parts sand.

3 The use of portland cement for stucco repair may cause the old material around the patch to powder and deteriorate. It is important when patching stucco to use as dry a mix as possible to avoid shrinking and cracking.

Structural reinforcement. The best time to correct problems in unreinforced masonry buildings is, of course, beforehand. An earthquake, however, sends a message that the time has come to take some steps, if financially feasible and if they can be carried out in a way that does not irreparably harm the historical or architectural integrity of a historic structure. Projecting parts and ornamentation may be most easily secured. Strengthening structural systems and anchoring walls, floors and roof remain as major retrofitting challenges anytime.

WOOD

Historic wooden buildings generally may be smaller than masonry ones, but they are in many ways no less complicated. After disaster strikes, the same general rules apply, with a few additional pointers:

1 Be sure that the building is fastened to its foundation, especially in earthquake-prone areas.

2 Tie together roof, walls and floors to strengthen the structural system.

3 Hesitate before making structural repairs or considering any demolition of the framing. Old wooden buildings tend to be overdesigned, meaning that they are stronger than modern ones of wood-frame construction. Much sound material thus may remain even though superficial damage or rot may be revealed in beams, for example.

4 Reinforce rotted or insect-infected beam ends by adding flitch plates, or "sisters."

5 Use metal or fiberglass bars to brace supporting components, protecting them with epoxy compounds.

6 Analyze mortise-and-tenon framing systems, which may be more vulnerable to stress than post-and-beam joining methods.

7 If the disaster recovery is used to upgrade the utilities in a historic structure, avoid drilling multiple holes through joists and beams, thus destroying or weakening the historic fabric.

WINDOWS AND DOORS

When nature gets extremely violent, wall openings such as windows and doors become just that — open. But these elements can be among the most important and decorative features in a historic building. If replacement of windows and doors is determined to be necessary, a partial replacement of components, such as the window sash alone, should be considered. If window or door frames are replaced, the exterior trim should closely match the original. With the glazing itself, the number of lights, or panes, and the thickness of the muntins, the dividing members, should be replicated. Repair may be easier than it looks.

1 Carefully remove broken glass panes from the sash to avoid breaking or further damaging glass that remains. Old putty may be softened using a heat gun or iron.

2 Consider repairing slightly cracked or broken glass panes, if old or decorative, with epoxy. In time, the epoxy may yellow if exposed to sunlight.

3 Use modern sheet glass for replacement panes in preference to imitation "old glass," which often contains an excess of bubbles and deformations.

4 Restore window sash by removing them from their channels and scraping away any loose putty. If necessary, take out all of the glazing compound, remove the panes and repair the muntins and frame. Fill minor holes with epoxy resins.

5 Correct moisture problems in a structure before repairing or replacing wooden trim. Elements in contact with damp masonry walls (more than 20 percent moisture content) will fail, and fungus or rot will almost certainly develop.

6 Never use an open flame or heat gun when working on wooden trim; both present a severe fire hazard.

PLASTER WALLS

In preparing the contents of a building for a disaster, furniture can be moved to upper stories or another location, paintings can be stored and archival materials can be relocated or covered in plastic. But historic walls have to stay in place and withstand wind, water or tremors. If water does infiltrate interior spaces, slow drying should be part of the immediate stabilization process. The first thing that historic plaster walls will do after a storm or earthquake is begin to crack. Once stabilized, or dried slowly, usually they can be restored using the following procedures:

1 Photograph damages to provide a detailed record to guide restoration.

2 Gradually dry wet or waterlogged plaster. Dehumidifiers or heaters may leach excessive moisture through the wall and thereby cause salts to crystalize in any material, whether plaster, stone or brick. The result will be a plaster surface that has lost all of its strength — it will become a powder.

3 Check plaster for firmness. If it is loose, reattachment with an acrylic plaster mix may be possible. This is a job for an expert.

4 Reattach plaster that has separated into layers, such as on ceilings, by installing screw buttons attached firmly in studs or joists. A stud finder will make this task much easier.

5 Save old plaster and its lath foundation. Even if the plaster is gone, old lath may prove useful in another part of a historic structure.

6 Patch hairline cracks with a thin mixture of plaster or wallboard joint compound. Rub the crack lightly with coarse sandpaper, brush out loose material and then force the filler deep into the crack, either with fingertips or a putty knife. Then smooth the repair with fine sandpaper.

7 Obtain professional assistance for larger cracks and extensive plaster repair such as entire walls and decorative elements.

RESTORATION HAZARDS

Special hazards come with postdisaster repair work, as they do with other restoration activities. Among the things to watch out for are:

1 Asbestos. Wind and water damage, as well as earthquake shaking, may cause asbestos fibers, which were used as insulation even into the early 1970s, to become airborne. If loose asbestos is detected on the site of a disaster, make sure that all work halts immediately and that professionals are brought in to clean it up.

2 Lead paint. Any stripping or scraping of paint on old buildings may uncover lead paint and release lead-contaminated dust, which is particularly poisonous to children. Equally dangerous is the use of heat guns or flames, which vaporize the lead in old paint.

3 Aftershocks. Continuing tremors and shakes can be dangerous to the safety of anyone working in a damaged building, especially doing structural repairs and using scaffolding.

LANDSCAPES

Trees and landscaping are as much a part of an area's character as its buildings, yet they are often more vulnerable to natural disasters than historic structures. Charleston, for example, in the aftermath of Hurricane Hugo was a changed area—its beloved canopy of trees denuded and its famous gardens in disarray. On the other hand, half a year after the catastrophic storm, in spring 1990, tourists and natives alike wondered in amazement at experiencing a city open to the sky much as Charleston had been a century earlier, before mature trees enshrouded it. A similar transformation occurred at Drayton Hall outside Charleston. The newly bare vista between the house and the Ashley River looks much as an octogenarian staff member recalled from his youth.

Rehabilitation. Landscapes are living, dynamic environments. Natural disasters may speed up the process of landscape change, but with skill and attention, they need not cause permanent damage. And storms such as Hugo also provide an opportunity for choice — for planning — in stabilizing the land-scape, protecting it and restoring it:

1 Immediately assess and document the damage with photographs and written statements.

2 Evaluate the condition and significance of any uprooted trees. Replant important trees that are capable of survival: prune them, remove damaged limbs, stand them upright (with stakes and cables for support) and give them growth hormones (fertilizers may burn weak roots).

3 Propagate damaged plant materials that cannot be rescued but are important landscape features; plant these as replacements when they are sufficiently hardy. Lost examples alternatively may be replaced with identical materials from nursery stock.

4 Exercise caution if using heavy equipment anywhere on the site, and especially when removing irretrievably damaged trees. Further damage to fragile plantings and archeological sites may occur. Consider using a crane or heli-copter for large trees.

5 Harvest fallen trees before they rot and become a fire or other hazard. Soft-woods must be harvested rapidly, preferably within several months. Hard-woods will last longer, perhaps two and one-half years. Plan well: because of prevailing weather conditions, harvesting may be feasible only during certain portions of the year.

6 Generally, replant all historic designed landscapes with historically appropriate materials that match the originals in species or cultivars (some antique cultivars may be hard, or impossible, to find); repair damaged structures; and replace destroyed items with replicas of the originals.

Restoration. Disaster recovery also presents an opportunity to assess the appropriateness of a landscape's previous form and condition. Did its most recent appearance, for example, correctly reflect its historical design and period? Was it overgrown or planted with inappropriate materials? Were planned vistas obscured?

These questions can be answered by researching the landscape's history and evolution, documenting existing conditions and then evaluating the conditions of all features, both plantings and structures such as buildings, water features and walkways. The restoration treatment should reestablish the historic spatial relationships of the landscape as well as its individual features, from plantings and land forms to furnishings such as benches, light fixtures and fountains. Disaster recovery also may bring an opportunity to upgrade mechanical and electrical systems, and to make the landscape accessible to handicapped visitors, as long as the historical character is retained.

Meeting Legal Requirements

They called it the Puerto Rican chain-saw massacre. Before Hurricane Hugo about 50 tall Australian pine trees lined the road to El Morro (1775–87), the historic fortress of San Juan. Immediately after the storm the trees were there, perhaps a little worse for wear. But several days later the trees were all gone, chopped down by the National Guard. The reason, said the superintendent of this National Historic Site, was that they were splintered and constituted a danger. The director of Puerto Rico's office of historic monuments offered a different explanation: the trees were cut down to take advantage of the opportunity presented by Hugo to restore the fort to how it looked under Spanish rule.

The action raised protests locally from students and residents who liked the shade that the trees had long provided, and it raised concerns nationally because landmark review procedures were not followed. El Morro is part of the National Park System (and a World Heritage Site), and as such, any federal actions affecting it are required to be reviewed and, if necessary, referred to the Advisory Council on Historic Preservation. "We don't endorse cutting down trees to restore a structure to its historic state," one council staff member told a newspaper when informed of the action.

In times of disaster, regulations protecting historic places sometimes are overlooked. Red-tagged landmark buildings may be summarily demolished, without proper review, and historic trees may be cut down, without proper review. Landmark review procedures, both local and federal, provide safeguards after a disaster just as they do in less stressful times.

LOCAL DESIGN REVIEW

About 2,000 cities and neighborhoods across the country have passed regulations providing for review of changes to designated landmarks and historic districts — exterior changes to facades and settings as well as the design of additions and new buildings. Appointed boards review applications at regular meetings and issue certificates of appropriateness if the plans are acceptable.

Charleston. After Hurricane Hugo, Charleston's Board of Architectural Review received three times the usual number of applications. The secretary of the board and city preservation officer, Charles Chase, later made the following recommendations based on his experience:

1 Do not lower your normal standards. Design and materials used in repairs remain important. Be strict about not approving inappropriate substitute materials, for example.

Restoring Order With Design Review

Once the dust has settled after a natural disaster, design review can provide an important protocol for putting buildings back into the mainstream.

First, because design review tends to be a public hearing on the status quo and proposed changes in a neighborhood, the very exercise restores a semblance of order just by considering the significance of damaged buildings and elements in a community context. A design review board serves as an authority that can prevent typical reflex actions — such as the urge to tear down and start over. The review process thus can stave off needless demolitions.

Second, design review makes possible a systematic analysis of what has occurred and why historic sites sometimes weather a storm better than new structures. This information has great educational value to others who have suffered similar damages.

Third, if thoughtfully conducted, design review can provide for the correct handling of the trickiest problems of all: the invisible ones, such as water-damaged plaster, that leave an undermined condition that will worsen with time and that, if badly repaired or undetected, can threaten a building and possibly the integrity of an entire historic district.

Finally, design review causes what is best about any democratic procedure to emerge — namely, whatever forms the core of common agreement. And, over time, it tends to raise the level of the debate, the shared concern and the collective appreciation of what is being preserved. There can be no more important time for these phenomena than after a natural disaster.

Adele Chatfield-Taylor, President
American Academy in Rome

2 Board procedures should not be compromised. If necessary increase the number of meetings and call on retired board members to serve as alternates for overworked members.

3 Waive review for temporary weatherization and stabilization measures if warranted, removing pressures to do more extensive work in a hurry. Provide public service announcements and publications and help guide such work.

4 Request engineering reports (paid for by owners) in support of demolition requests; reports must prove that deficiencies necessitate such drastic action.

5 Use neighborhood residents or a neighborhood association to act as monitors for potential violations, then inspect referred sites.

6 Be sure that the landmarks inventory is current; update photographs when changes are approved by the board.

The board also became involved in monitoring contractors as an additional means of helping guarantee quality rehabilitation. Every worker was fingerprinted and issued a city identification card. Outside contractors especially were supervised, given their lack of familiarity with city codes and building techniques.

San Francisco. Across the country, the Landmarks Preservation Advisory Board of San Francisco wrestled with a similar onrush of projects requiring review. It took a number of key steps to smooth the process:

1 Prepared a policy statement reaffirming preservation principles and procedures, sending copies to key officials and offices such as the mayor, building and fire departments, redevelopment agency and port authority.

2 Agreed to meet weekly to handle applications — and daily as needed to process requests involving buildings tagged red (unsafe to enter) and yellow (safe on a limited basis).

3 Notified landmark owners about the ongoing review and permit process, providing a list of professionals ready to give assistance. In historic districts, volunteers distributed materials door-to-door.

4 Obtained the official daily list of inspected buildings citywide to determine which ones were landmarks.

5 Established priorities for designated landmarks to receive second opinions on the inspection results.

6 Waived permit fees.

7 Assisted with permit processing in other city departments.

8 Supported owner applications for emergency funds through programs such as FEMA and the SBA.

9 Cooperated with private groups, including the local preservation organization and National Trust regional office, to prepare resource lists and send out expert preservation evaluation teams.

10 Recommended as a postquake priority the completion of the citywide historic resources survey, creation of a landmarks database and development with others of preparedness programs such as publications, workshops and inspection services.

Sullivan's Island, S.C. In South Carolina many counties, unlike the city of Charleston, have no land use or landmarks controls at all, often because of intense opposition. A case study of Sullivan's Island, north of Charleston, prepared for the National Trust after Hugo provides an example of how local design review, whether legislated procedures or voluntary guidelines, can facilitate the recovery of communities.

Fifteen percent of the island's documented historic structures were destroyed by the hurricane. But even before the storm, residents had been aware that inappropriate, often larger-scale construction was creeping in. Rising real estate values had pressured property owners to upgrade, enlarge or replace the simple beach structures that define the township's historical character. But no consensus had emerged as to how to deal with the situation. Twice in two years the planning and zoning commission had voted in favor of creating a historic district, which both times was rejected by the town council. The problems on Sullivan's Island—the threat of new development, differing attitudes about the merit of design controls, arguments over private property rights and the ways in which public opinion can be mobilized—are similar to those throughout the country.

The issue came to a head because of the volume of post-Hugo rebuilding. The hurricane also hardened attitudes against architectural and design review as a mandated process—after the storm, citizens spoke out 10-to-1 against the proposed historic district ordinance. The National Trust sponsored a workshop to showcase how design standards pioneered by architects Elizabeth Plater-Zyberk and Andrés Duany might apply to Sullivan's Island. Several points emerged:

1 Conflicting government goals can heighten design and planning problems, such as prohibiting residential use of outbuildings that would provide affordable housing.

2 Parking is a major problem that leads to others, such as inappropriate private fences to screen out stray vehicles, trash and noise.

3 Opposition to controls need not preclude development of voluntary guidelines.

4 Continued discussion of preservation values may raise consciousness in the community. Opposition to controls may decrease when homeowners realize that continued degradation of historic structures is having a corresponding effect on the economic value of their properties.

SECTION 106 REVIEW

The cities and towns most heavily affected by the Loma Prieta earthquake, from San Francisco and Oakland to San Jose and Santa Cruz, have more than 2,000 historic properties listed in or eligible for the National Register of Historic Places. South Carolina has 8,700 nationally designated historic resources, including 4,500 in the Charleston area. North Carolina's National Register sites total more than 4,600, the Virgin Islands 2,000 and Puerto Rico some 800. In addition to such recognized historic places, many more that have not been listed, but are or may be eligible, exist throughout the country — an estimated 90,000 or more in Hugo's path alone.

Advisory Council on Historic Preservation. Under Section 106 of the National Historic Preservation Act of 1966, the Advisory Council on Historic Preservation is authorized to review federal actions affecting properties listed in or eligible for the National Register of Historic Places. Included in the definition of federal actions is work carried out directly by federal agencies as well as funded and licensed projects. Federal agencies are required to review potential historic properties likely to be affected by an undertaking and determine if their actions will have no effect, no adverse effect or will instead produce some harm — in a disaster this can range from inappropriate rehabilitation to outright demolition. Agencies work with state historic preservation offices in making such findings and seeking ways to mitigate the damage, if any. Only if an agreement cannot be reached is the matter referred to the council for comment. The federal agency makes the final determination of whether and how to proceed.

Federal Emergency Management Agency. In a natural disaster, the federal agency most likely to be involved with historic buildings is the Federal Emergency Management Agency, given its role in providing rehabilitation funding. While FEMA has tackled preservation review requirements in past disasters, the one-two punch of the 1989 catastrophes has spurred it to work more closely with the council and other preservationists to develop the best possible procedures for historic properties in an emergency. The agency stresses that its role differs noticeably from most other federal programs because its aid, and thus its review process, comes after the fact — a disaster — rather than in project planning stages.

The Loma Prieta experience. Over the years FEMA has developed its own procedures for complying with Section 106, acknowledging its responsibility to take into account the effects of its financial aid programs on historic properties. The agency, in cooperation with California's state historic preservation office and Office of Emergency Services, developed steps governing demolitions after the Loma Prieta earthquake, to come into play after a 30-day emergency period when FEMA or OES was notified that a historic property was to be demolished and that an application for reimbursement of demolition costs was to be filed. The agency:

1 Inspected damaged property to evaluate whether it was historic — 50 years or older.

2 If the property was considered historic, FEMA determined whether immediate demolition was necessary.

3 If so, removal of the property was allowed to proceed without delay.

4 FEMA agreed to provide the SHPO, within 60 days after the emergency period, with a list of all historic properties that were demolished during the period.

5 FEMA agreed, if it determined that immediate demolition was not necessary, to provide the SHPO and Advisory Council on Historic Preservation with a basic description of the property and its condition and afford the SHPO and council seven days in which to comment on the proposed demolition. FEMA said that it would consider their comments in reaching a final decision concerning demolition. FEMA added that failure of the SHPO and council to respond within seven days would not prohibit it from recommending demolition of the property. The agency also supported the costs of hiring a consulting engineer with experience in historic buildings.

Some confusion about the procedures arose, notably that some officials and property owners interpreted them to mean that to obtain FEMA aid, their properties had to be torn down in the 30-day emergency period during which normal review procedures were suspended. An extended memorandum of agreement was soon signed by the original agencies, and a FEMA representative remained in California long after the quake, reviewing funding applications for historic properties. Overall, about 750 cases were examined in the state, with 10 that could not be resolved locally referred to the council; a similar number reached the council in Hugo's wake. In the previous and less-severe 1987 Whittier, Calif., earthquake, about 35 funded structures were reviewed with the SHPO, and three were sent on to the council for comment.

Financing Disaster Recovery

Just as there will never be a shortage of preservation projects, there will always be a shortage of funds. In disasters as in normal times, preservation projects have to compete with a universe of worthwhile needs, some of them much more dramatic life-and-death matters of public safety and health. Surveyed here are some existing financial-aid programs as well as examples of special funds used after Hugo and Loma Prieta. The 1989 disasters produced recommendations specifically addressing ways to provide better disaster financing; a number of them are outlined among the recommendations in the following chapter, Preparing for the Next Disaster.

FEDERAL ASSISTANCE

The Federal Emergency Management Agency and Small Business Administration provide most of the interim financing for repairs to historic buildings after disasters. Both FEMA and SBA cover only damages above those underwritten by private insurance. FEMA's assistance takes the form of grants, while SBA makes loans.

Federal Emergency Management Agency. FEMA heavily emphasizes restoring the functions of government and such needs as housing, utility and road repairs, unemployment assistance and crisis counseling. Its grant programs (75 percent federally funded, 25 percent state or local) cover:

1 Stabilization, repair, rehabilitation or replacement of public facilities.

2 Stabilization, repair, rehabilitation or replacement of private nonprofit facilities such as schools, libraries, hospitals and museums, but not churches.

3 Demolition expenses, including buildings on private property.

4 Debris removal and erection of scaffolding or fencing to lessen threats to the public.

5 Individual and family grants. This program is available only to individuals and families who are unable to qualify for SBA assistance. Grants are limited to $10,000 and provide 75 percent of the actual cost of meeting necessary expenses or serious needs.

The FEMA regulations include a section affecting historic properties, addressing the issue of repair versus replacement. They state that a property is eligible for full replacement to "a functionally equivalent but not identical facility" when repair costs equal or exceed 50 percent of the cost of replacement. Applicants may instead elect to repair rather than replace the property, but eligible costs are limited to the less expensive of the two options. And "replacement" does not encompass restoration to the original appearance. FEMA's practice has been to replace the functional capacity of a property but not necessarily to restore its historic features. Thus, its aid is available not for authentic restoration but only to help pay for costs necessary to return buildings to an operable condition; only for the costs of repairs and replacement of a similar-size structure; and only for exterior and structural work, not collections inside a building.

Small Business Administration. SBA programs provide:

1 Low-interest loans of up to $100,000 for repair or replacement of a primary residence, including landscaping and recreational facilities.

2 Low-interest loans of up to $20,000 for repair or replacement of household and personal property. Both homeowners and renters are eligible.

3 Low-interest loans of up to $500,000 for business owners and nonprofit organizations to repair, rehabilitate or replace their property.

With the 1989 disasters in mind, preservationists recommended a number of changes in FEMA and SBA procedures. For one, they urged that FEMA create a special category for historic properties with funds specifically allocated to cover the extra costs involved in returning a historic structure to its predisaster condition. It was also suggested that FEMA and SBA staff be trained in the special requirements of historic properties, including the work and costs required to inspect and restore them.

Internal Revenue Service. In the aftermath of Hurricane Hugo and the Loma Prieta earthquake, the IRS came through for owners of historic properties. Because of the twin disasters, it ruled that sudden, unexpected and nonrecurring events were deductible against current income, retroactively to 1986. Previously, property owners, including historic property owners, had to wait until selling before claiming the losses that natural disasters can bring.

National Park Service. In response to the 1989 disasters, the Park Service allocated all available monies from the Historic Preservation Fund to the affected state historic preservation offices. In addition, funding received through the President's Discretionary Fund for Disaster Relief was made available in the five states and territories for assessment, stabilization and repair of significant damaged historic properties. The agency would like to secure authority in future emergencies to rapidly redirect portions of the Historic Preservation Fund appropriations to meet emergency needs.

Independent Agencies. Other federal programs that support preservation projects generally may be able to offer special aid, particularly in planning for disasters.

1 The National Endowment for the Arts financed historic-property damage assessment studies in 1989 and 1990 carried out by the National Trust. NEA's Care of Collections Program also offers potential for special conservation training workshops, security and disaster proofing. Other categories support fellowships and special challenge grants.

2 The National Endowment for the Humanities, which focuses on libraries and archival materials, has no specific category for disasters but accepts related applications under its Office of Preservation Programs. It is considering involvement in establishing a network of regional conservation centers.

3 The Institute of Museum Services also has no emergency aid programs but has funded conservation-planning workshops. It generally serves as a clearinghouse for museums, including those that may be developing disaster plans and want to share ideas with others.

STATE ASSISTANCE

The 1989 disasters provide examples of how states can help underwrite recovery costs. Using funds from the Historic Preservation Fund, administered by the National Park Service, and the president's discretionary fund, states and territories involved in Hugo and Loma Prieta were able to make grants for assessment, stabilization and repair through their state historic preservation offices. Drawing on a $100,000 fund, South Carolina offered special weatherization grants of $5,000 for historic structures. Following the earthquake, the California legislature furnished near-immediate financial assistance. In a marathon three-day session, the legislature enacted, among other bills, laws providing $74 million in disaster recovery assistance. The state also received $200,000 from the president's discretionary fund. Housing assistance specifically called for consideration of the historical nature of a structure.

Other state sources that support preservation projects generally include passage of bond issues for preservation; special state taxes, such as land transfer taxes, that may be increased for preservation purposes; state housing authority support of historic neighborhood preservation; state councils on the arts and humanities; and publicly supported statewide revolving funds.

LOCAL ASSISTANCE

Typical local programs that aid preservation include appropriations of local government agencies; tax exemptions, fee waivers and abatements; local government underwriting of loans or principal-reduction grants; city distributions of community development block grants, a federal grant program; spe-

One often overlooked effect of the 1989 earthquake was the major blow it leveled on low-income housing. In Santa Cruz County alone more than 600 units were lost, 400 of them in historic buildings. Many of these old structures provided housing for children and senior citizens, among others. Before the quake the Casa del Rey Hotel was home to 180 elderly residents; afterward, it was condemned and demolished. Downtown, in the Pacific Garden Mall Historic District, the Palomar Inn was damaged but later repaired and reopened to its 97 senior-citizen tenants. The St. George Hotel, which had 150 low-income residents, became the center of a heated preservation battle, complete with arson, and was demolished a year after the earthquake.

Some rehabilitation efforts were more successful. In Watsonville the Stag and Resetar hotels were quickly made habitable within a few days. The 36-room Jefsen Hotel, a downtown landmark, was purchased by a nonprofit developer for rehabilitation. Despite its configuration, with small units above a commercial block, the hotel was occupied by many families.

The loss of low-income housing — also significant in San Francisco and Alameda counties — will be a devastating problem for these communities for years to come. Single residents have had a far more difficult time receiving continued disaster aid than have families: many remained without permanent shelter or had to move to places with higher rents. A year after the earthquake, plans for low-cost replacements for only 307 of the 610 lost units had been announced — with the first to be completed two years after the 1989 disaster.

Kathleen Stratton, Paralegal Advocate, Housing Law Center
Legal Aid Society of Santa Cruz County

cial local taxes; local government designation of a portion of general obligation or special-assessment bond funds; and annual state preservation appropriations for Certified Local Governments under the National Historic Preservation Act of 1966.

As a potential model for other cities, San Jose, Calif., responded to the Loma Prieta earthquake by proposing a package of incentives to retrofit commercial and residential buildings for seismic protection. Recipients would include about 200 designated historic structures, buildings that contribute to a historic district and others that fit into the city's retail strategy.

PRIVATE ASSISTANCE

National Trust for Historic Preservation. With funds specially contributed by its members as well as grants from the National Endowment for the Arts, the National Trust initiated detailed survey efforts to investigate the scope of damages following Hugo and Loma Prieta. The Trust also reached out to individual historic property owners with financial help, both directly from the Trust and by putting them in touch with financial-aid agencies. The California experience provides a good example:

1 The National Trust sponsored an emergency stabilization loan program, in partnership with local foundations and banks located in areas affected by the earthquake, providing low-interest, short-term loans for property stabilization. Red-tagged buildings were given priority.

2 With funding provided by the President's Discretionary Fund for Disaster Relief, the National Trust also made grants of up to $5,000 to governments, nonprofit organizations and private property owners for professional assistance in planning rehabilitation of historic structures. Projects eligible for the program included rehabilitation plans for homeowners who experienced extensive damage, including recovery and cost estimates; feasibility studies for commercial property owners to estimate costs and procedures for returning properties to productive use, with seismic retrofitting; conferences and workshops that might focus, for example, on design guidelines for new, infill construction; and studies of ways to retrofit individual unreinforced masonry buildings.

3 It additionally cooperated, through its National Main Street Center and other offices, in supplying consulting services by designers and engineers to California Main Street communities, working with the California Department of Commerce. The objective was to assess the habitability of specific downtown properties and address design and cost issues involved in rebuilding commercial structures.

4 With generous support from the Hewlett Foundation, the Trust's Western Regional Office began an ongoing program providing technical assistance to earthquake-damaged buildings.

State and local private funds. Common sources of private support are membership dues and budgets of preservation organizations; donations; private revolving funds; funds from banks and saving institutions under the Community Reinvestment Act or disaster-response programs; joint ventures with for-profit and government entities; local foundations and corporations; and special events such as house tours and sales of preservation-related products.

How Did We Do? Postdisaster Evaluation

Any emergency, up through a full-fledged natural disaster, provides a learning experience, from evaluating the effectiveness of a formal emergency plan to assessing how everyone performed under pressure. In fact, a postemergency critique should be part of the recovery process for each historic property, city and state or other affected institution.

The J. Paul Getty Museum in earthquake-prone Malibu, Calif., has developed a set of evaluation questions that can be adapted by others and asked of all the participants:

Cause. What were the major contributing factors of the emergency or disaster?

Notification. Were you given timely notice of the emergency? Of your assigned role? How were you notified and by whom? Were you given accurate and adequate information? How can notification procedures be improved?

Communications. What methods of communication were used: telephones, runners, radios, other? If you are a manager or supervisor, did you receive a radio? Did you use it? Were the communications effective?

Collections management. Did the damage mitigation procedures and salvage operations reduce or prevent water damage, fire damage, etc.? How could these operations be improved? Were conservation efforts well coordinated and prioritized? Were adequate personnel available? Were they effectively deployed? Were art movement and temporary storage arrangements well planned and well handled? What kinds of specialized conservation tools and supplies were needed that were not available? Were they obtained? Did the delay play a significant role in the outcome of the incident? Was art damage and art movement documented in a timely manner? Were photographs taken? Was the incident videotaped?

Control room operations. Were operations effective? Were control communications clear and concise? Were communications timely? Were events documented? Were appropriate personnel assigned to the control room immediately? How can procedures be improved?

Protective services. Were the security and safety of staff and visitors properly considered? Was the appropriate pool of equipment and supplies established? Were adequate personnel available? Were personnel well deployed? Were all operations conducted in a safe manner? Did personnel use safe methods and equipment? What kinds of equipment or supplies were needed that were not available? Were they obtained? Did the delay play a significant role in the outcome of the incident? Did all equipment operate properly? Was security of collections, buildings and grounds maintained?

Media relations. Were the media contacted? Did the media contact the museum? Did those staff in touch with the media give only appropriate information? How can such contacts be improved?

Action checklists. Did you use an action checklist? Was it useful? How can it be improved?

Unexpected contingencies. Were there any special circumstances or serious unexpected problems? Were they handled appropriately? What other problems could have arisen? How could they have been handled?

Overall effectiveness of the emergency plan. Was an emergency declared and did someone take charge? Was a chain of command established, clearly understood and followed? Were duties delegated to the appropriate people and the necessary adjustments made? Were major decisions and activities documented?

Recommendations and conclusions. How could the incident have been avoided? Damage lessened? Which policies and procedures need reevaluation? What specific lessons were learned in this incident?

PREPARING FOR THE NEXT DISASTER

Recommendations for Action

Preparing for the next disaster
may prevent unnecessary losses.
Santa Cruz's historic St. George Hotel
was damaged by the 1989 earthquake,
later victimized by arson
and eventually demolished.
(Bill Lovejoy, *San Jose Mercury News*)

THE OUTCOME of an earthquake "is

determined before the ground starts shaking," William Medigovich, director of California's Office of Emergency Services, told the Senate Subcommittee on Science, Space and Technology in 1989. This statement is as true of other natural disasters as it is of earthquakes. What, then, must preservationists and public officials do to protect historic places in future natural disasters? To reiterate a point made many times in this book, it is not a question of whether disasters will occur, but when.

Learn from the past. Disaster planners and preservationists would do well to keep the lessons of Hurricane Hugo and the Loma Prieta earthquake constantly in mind. These emergencies demonstrated the value of planning for disasters and maintaining — as well as, where needed, strengthening — historic places. The studies commissioned by the National Trust in the wake of 1989's natural disasters, on the Virgin Islands, Puerto Rico, the Carolinas and California, in particular contain recommendations for action that, when viewed together, distill ways of keeping harm at a minimum in future calamities.

Make a commitment. Preparedness requires commitment: of individual and staff time; of government policy at the federal, state and local levels; of professional experts, national and local organizations, property owners, volunteers; and of money.

Plan ahead. Preparing emergency plans and carrying out mitigating procedures hold the most promise for safeguarding historic places. Otherwise, business as usual will prevail. The most important thing to do is plan ahead.

Before Disaster Strikes

Historic site managers, government planning officials, homeowners — anyone with responsibility for emergency situations — should have a written plan of action for different disaster types and intensities. Plans should incorporate both actions to take in emergencies as well as measures that can be implemented immediately to mitigate against unpreventable losses. Plans should be reviewed periodically. For historic property owners, such readiness may mean maintaining the property and rotating adequate supplies; for the government planner, it may mean having mobilization plans for engineers and architects qualified to evaluate historic resources.

No one can foresee all potential disaster circumstances. Plans should be kept simple, adaptable and flexible. The difficult part for the person or committee preparing a plan will be imagining and anticipating the stress and psychological dislocation that accompany disaster. The preparedness plan will spell out priorities and responsibilities and detail specific actions to be taken when clear-headed thinking is likely to be impaired.

RECOMMENDATIONS

1 Assess the hazards, vulnerabilities and risks inherent in likely disasters. Remember that fires are probably the most common and most easily preventable of all disasters.

2 Survey and inventory individual sites, collections and broader community historic resources. Survey results must be accessible and are best computerized.

3 Create an emergency preparedness plan in writing for individual houses, public and commercial buildings, museums, other historic structures as well as towns, counties and states. Make sure that it is updated regularly, has a clear chain of command and is kept in a secure place.

4 Develop an emergency local or regional network drawing together appropriate public and private players. Specify procedures for interacting with other organizations and government offices.

5 Plan for the aftermath of an emergency, making no assumptions about the availability of water, electricity, telephone service or other amenities of modern life.

6 Regularly inspect and maintain the integrity of historic structures and landscapes. Use as your motto "Maintain, maintain, maintain," especially for historic structures in the path of any natural disaster. In seismic zones, explore financial support for retrofitting.

7 Establish special planning measures for collections, recognizing that some parts are more valuable than others; develop a list of priority items.

8 Train staffs of historic house museums, preservation organizations and local governments in how the plan works, including practice drills.

9 Educate the public and media on the importance of historic buildings, maintenance, disaster preparedness and recovery techniques.

10 Use the effects of natural disasters to help interpret historic structures and landscapes as part of a public education program.

During a Disaster

Here planning, again, is the most important and effective activity. An earthquake, of course, provides no warning at all, tornadoes little and hurricanes a few days at most; therefore, taking action beforehand that will allow a timely response to the disaster's likely effects will pay off. A trip to the local convenience store to buy fresh radio batteries may require only minutes, but with fallen trees and impassable roads after a disaster the same journey may take hours, and the store probably will be closed.

RECOMMENDATIONS

1 Remember that human safety and welfare come first.

2 Using a previously identified network of qualified public and private sources, inventory and document damages with checklists, written descriptions and photographs, to guide funding, restoration and insurance claims.

3 Move quickly to stabilize and weatherize damaged structures and secure sites against possible vandalism, either deliberate or inadvertent, during cleanup.

4 Manage disaster response from a central, preferably office-equipped location.

5 Be constantly aware of the "do something now" mentality that comes naturally with disasters, and counsel patience and a "second opinion" before irreversible action or demolition is undertaken on a historic structure. Monitor public inspection teams and offer assistance.

6 Mobilize people and resources based on priorities, such as the most important and most damaged sites.

7 Draw from a list of qualified persons or experts with special skills for the evaluation and stabilization work, and quickly seek professional expertise for collections such as furnishings, artwork, objects, books and papers. Develop clear tasks for volunteers.

8 Ensure that landmark protection and design review procedures are not suspended or reduced in the emergency. Government plans should include emergency procedures for such review.

9 Communicate with the public through the media or special means such as flyers and workshops, and require someone to be in charge of public relations.

10 Be aware that disasters may reveal opportunities for important historical research that otherwise could not occur.

After a Disaster

Recovery from a disaster is an exercise in frustration, regardless of the amount of planning done or stockpiles accumulated. Supplies of essential items will be short; numbers of skilled workers will be even shorter; funding may be complicated to obtain. For all concerned, this situation counsels patience and perseverance: do what must be done to stabilize and secure historic places, then take good time to make repairs and rehabilitation right. A long-term recovery schedule will involve actions ranging from immediate to five or more years in the future.

RECOMMENDATIONS

1 Be sure that the stabilization and initial repair processes do no further harm to damaged places.

2 Dry any wet structures and collections slowly and carefully. For structures, radical changes in moisture levels may be more harmful than moisture itself.

3 Wait for skilled labor and historically appropriate materials before starting detailed restoration.

4 Maintain usual preservation standards, following local and national guidelines.

5 Adhere to design review procedures to ensure that postdisaster work does not change historic features or materials.

6 If demolition is necessary to ensure safety, keep it to a minimum and do it carefully. Elements removed from historic structures should not be discarded; carefully store them for reuse during restoration.

7 Replant uprooted landscape features such as trees that can survive. Protect all surviving plant materials by using extreme care with heavy equipment.

8 Spread the word that funds exist for emergency stabilization and historically appropriate rehabilitation.

9 Keep the public informed about your progress.

10 Focus on regaining revenue sources if business has been interrupted.

11 Review how everyone involved performed in the emergency.

12 Update your emergency plan to learn from the experience.

Public Policies

Both Hurricane Hugo and the Loma Prieta earthquake demonstrated an urgent need for reform in public policies on disasters—particularly to protect historic places. Current policies that rely on waiting for a disaster to happen, and paying for it later, have been found to make neither political nor fiscal sense. Because natural disasters are going to happen, and when they do governments are going to be involved in paying for the damages, the public has a direct and vital interest in keeping injury—to populations and structures—to a minimum. Paying the bill now to reduce disaster risks is a small investment that will pay off when the next disaster comes.

The 1989 events gave rise to a number of conclusions regarding public policy for historic properties during emergencies:

1 A strong public policy in favor of preservation should be developed in a number of ways, including integrating preservation concerns into local emergency planning procedures and ordinances; establishing rehabilitation standards for historic buildings; and surveying historic resources.

2 The psychological effects of disasters must be understood, including the fact that public officials may be preoccupied with protecting the safety of their citizens and property owners may be in states of shock, unable to make rational decisions about safeguarding their properties.

3 Economic factors enter into postdisaster decisions; for example, owners with economically marginal historic buildings may not be prepared to take on more debt.

4 Economic incentives are needed—preferably before the next disaster and certainly afterward—to ensure the appropriate treatment of historic places.

The studies supported by the National Trust following the 1989 disasters recommended a range of public policy initiatives, including the following, that can be implemented through legislation, regulations and administrative actions:

LOCAL

Preservation. Assume a preservation position, taking all reasonable steps to prevent the loss of historic buildings without endangering public safety. Incorporate preservation into disaster plans. Know which policies and regulations will be in force during a disaster. Work in cooperation with networks of preservationists.

Information. Conduct comprehensive historic resource surveys, complete with thorough photographic documentation. Integrate data into local records such as zoning documents, property lists, city maps. Place information in a secure, accessible location.

Design and technical. Encourage maintenance and appropriate retrofitting measures, offering financial aid or incentives. Locate structural engineers and other experts qualified to assess damages caused by disasters. Require proof of instability or economic hardship before allowing postdisaster demolitions. Streamline permitting procedures in emergencies to encourage repair over demolition. Stabilize or place liens on properties if owners fail to act. If historic buildings are lost, require sympathetic replacements, changing zoning if necessary.

Financial. Offer financial aid or incentives for retrofitting before a disaster and rehabilitation afterward. Encourage low-interest loan pools through private lenders. Use existing bond mechanisms, redevelopment agencies and other local programs. Provide tax rebates for upgrading buildings. Waive fees for repair permits during emergencies. Create grant programs. Retain experts to provide professional services. Acquire endangered properties by eminent domain or urge their sale to a preservation-minded buyer. Encourage repair of historic commercial buildings to avoid economic dislocations and loss of business.

Legal. Maintain existing preservation and environmental review procedures during an emergency, modifying steps if necessary without reducing standards. Ensure that state and federal regulations are followed.

Educational. Communicate local preservation and disaster policies to residents, particularly historic property owners. Clarify the role of citizens in working with the government to carry out policies. Provide publications and other guidance in preservation techniques and procedures. Conduct emergency preparedness drills.

STATE

Emergency procedures. Incorporate protection for historic properties into disaster plans. Develop means of cooperation among appropriate state agencies including the emergency and preservation offices, as well as with other preservationists.

Preservation. Increase personal, professional and financial resources available for emergencies in the state historic preservation offices. Complete statewide surveys and make them available to disaster teams; require survey grant recipients to regularly update and file survey information.

Building codes. Review building codes to ensure that they include clear and appropriate strengthening requirements for historic structures. Develop a model local building code ordinance providing suitable treatments for historic buildings. Disseminate information to facilitate compliance.

Environmental review. Develop alternative preservation protections for emergency periods when normal landmarks and other review processes may be suspended. Clarify vaguenesses such as the length of the emergency period and the responsibilities of local or federal governments.

Economic. Assess economic impacts of disasters, including costs of preparedness measures as well as long-term effects of historic buildings lost in disasters (such as reduced tourism and business). Channel existing financial programs and develop emergency funds to help in emergencies. Offer income tax credits for retrofitting and loans for rehabilitation of hazardous buildings. Increase the state match available for FEMA grants involving historic properties. Use state Main Street programs to ensure the continued viability of historic downtowns after disasters.

Insurance. Develop a state disaster insurance program for all types of historic buildings, based on risk-pooling principles similar to the federal flood insurance program and ones now available in Texas and California. Offer low rates and deductibles plus incentives for retrofitting.

State properties. Plan and budget for emergencies, including maintenance, strengthening and recovery.

NATIONAL

The Advisory Council on Historic Preservation has proposed that a prototype planning exercise begin with a cross section of interested federal, state and local agencies as well as organizations from the private sector. Its program development report, *Disaster Management Program: Protecting Historic Resources at Risk*, presents a series of actions designed to prevent damage to property and protect lives in all natural disasters.

General recommendations. The council identified four major areas to pursue:

1 Identification of the historic resources in the United States at risk from natural disasters

2 Development of an integrated planning program for federal, state and local jurisdictions, designed to provide guidance to users on risks, treatments and administration

3 Creation of a nationwide historic resources disaster management network to help coordinate such a program

4 Sponsorship of public education and training programs

Model proposal. Because prevention is the best medicine for historic structures, the council recommended that a computer-aided design and planning program be implemented to bring together government and private officials who would be involved in disaster relief efforts. "It is possible with some accuracy," the council's report says, "to define those geographic areas that are at greatest risk from natural disasters, those historic resources that may be affected, including those that may be destroyed or damaged, and establish treatment recommendations for retrofitting existing historic buildings to withstand damage."

This program, if funded and implemented, would provide in readily accessible form that most scarce of postdisaster commodities: information for decision makers. The council proposes that the Federal Emergency Management Agency take the lead in funding and developing the system, which would be created initially as a pilot program involving four areas—California, the central Mississippi River valley, the Gulf Coast of Texas and coastal South Carolina—and two disaster types—hurricanes and earthquakes.

Program components. Initially the six-part program would:

1 Identify historic resources at risk from natural disasters

2 Identify the types of disasters posing risks and the level of risk to families of resources, such as load-bearing masonry buildings, as well as individual resources, based on location and type of construction

3 Establish guidelines for retrofitting historic resources to prevent or minimize damage in case of a disaster

4 Establish guidelines for treatment of resources in case of disaster, including postdisaster survey techniques

5 Identify administrative procedures to be followed in a disaster

6 Assign a risk level (from 0 to 4) to each resource or family of resources. Levels of risk would be defined by the type of natural disaster, probability of disaster, probable level of damage and significance of the resource

Program participants. The council has proposed a list of organizations that should be involved in the program (some of them at later stages):

Advisory Council on Historic Preservation
U.S. Army Corps of Engineers, Construction
    Engineering Research Laboratory
Department of Veterans Affairs

Department of the Army
Department of Commerce, U.S. Geological Survey
Federal Emergency Management Agency
General Services Administration

National Park Service, U.S. Department of the Interior, including the disaster management office, National Register of Historic Places, Historic American Buildings Survey/Historic American Engineering Record, Golden Gate National Recreation Area and Padre Island National Seashore

National Science Foundation

National Trust for Historic Preservation

Congressional Office of Technology Assessment

National Conference of State Historic Preservation Officers

California State Historic Preservation Office

Missouri State Historic Preservation Office

South Carolina State Historic Preservation Office

Texas State Historic Preservation Office

City of Charleston, S.C.

City of Galveston, Tex.

City of St. Louis

City of San Francisco

American Society for Testing of Materials

American Institute of Architects

American Society of Professional Engineers

Construction Specifications Institute

Association for Preservation Technology

American Society of Civil Engineers

Products. Potential outcomes of the program include:

1 Published, comprehensive identification and analysis of historic resources that are subject to natural disasters, with recommended protective and corrective actions

2 Series of published reports of historic resources classified by federal agency and state

3 Computer program shell for public agencies to use in developing their own special disaster management programs

4 Disaster management network through the Cultural Resources Information Bulletin Board at the U.S. Army Construction Engineering Research Laboratory in Champaign, Ill.

5 Training programs for different groups from government officials to property managers, owners, and school and university students

Investment for the Future

Hurricane Hugo, the Loma Prieta earthquake, and countless fires and storms have demonstrated time and time again that protecting historic places from natural disasters begins with anticipating and preparing for their inevitable occurrence. The more that can be done now to prepare for the next disaster, the greater the savings in lives and costs. America's historic heritage, and future generations of Americans, deserves the investment.

Where To Get Help

The organizations listed in this section provide a variety of services, ranging from expertise on preservation, conservation and disaster recovery to financial aid. Good places to begin seeking disaster planning assistance include the appropriate state historic preservation offices and statewide preservation organizations, both listed below.

Federal Programs

Advisory Council on Historic Preservation
1100 Pennsylvania Avenue, N.W., Suite 803
Washington, D.C. 20506
(202) 786-0503

Federal Emergency Management Agency
500 C Street, S.W.
Washington, D.C. 20472
(202) 646-3484

Institute of Museum Services
1100 Pennsylvania Avenue, N.W., Suite 510
Washington, D.C. 20506
(202) 786-0539

Library of Congress
National Preservation Program, LMG-07
Washington, D.C. 20540
(202) 707-1840

National Endowment for the Arts
1100 Pennsylvania Avenue, N.W.
Washington, D.C. 20506
(202) 682-5442

National Endowment for the Humanities
Office of Preservation
1100 Pennsylvania Avenue, N.W.
Washington, D.C. 20506
(202) 786-0570

National Historical Publications and
Records Commission
National Archives Building
Washington, D.C. 20408
(202) 501-5610

Smithsonian Institution
Office of Risk Management
Washington, D.C. 20560
(202) 287-3338

U.S. Department of the Interior
National Park Service
P.O. Box 37127
Washington, D.C. 20013-7127

Curatorial Services Division
(202) 343-8142

Historic American Buildings Survey/
Historic American Engineering Record
(202) 343-9606

National Register of Historic Places
(202) 343-9536

Park Historic Architecture Division
(202) 343-8146

Preservation Assistance Division
(202) 343-9573

U.S. Geological Survey
905 National Center
Reston, Va. 22092
(703) 648-6711

National Organizations

Alliance for Historic Landscape
Preservation
82 Wall Street, Suite 1105
New York, N.Y. 10005
(617) 491-3727

American Association for State and Local
History
172 Second Avenue, North, Suite 102
Nashville, Tenn. 37201
(615) 255-2971

American Association of Museums
1225 I Street, N.W., Suite 200
Washington, D.C. 20005
(202) 238-1818

American Institute for Conservation of
Historic and Artistic Works
1400 16th Street, N.W., Suite 340
Washington, D.C. 20036
(202) 232-6636

American Institute of Architects
Community Assistance Initiative
1735 New York Avenue, N.W.
Washington, D.C. 20006
(202) 626-7300

American Society of Civil Engineers
345 East 47th Street
New York, N.Y. 10017
(212) 705-7671

American Society of Landscape Architects
4401 Connecticut Avenue, N.W.
Fifth Floor
Washington, D.C. 20008-2302
(202) 686-2752

American Society of Mechanical Engineers
345 East 47th Street
New York, N.Y. 10017
(212) 705-7740

Applied Technology Council
3 Twin Dolphin Drive, Suite 275
Redwood City, Calif. 94065-1595
(415) 595-1542

Archeological Conservancy
415 Orchard Drive
Santa Fe, N.M. 87501
(505) 982-3278

Association for Preservation Technology
International
904 Princess Anne Street
P.O. Box 8178
Fredericksburg, Va. 22404
(703) 373-1621

Bay Area Regional Earthquake
Preparedness Project
101 Eighth Street, Suite 152
Oakland, Calif. 94607
(415) 893-0818

Center for Preservation and Rehabilitation
Technology
College of Architecture and Urban Studies
Virginia Polytechnic Institute and
State University
201 Cowgill Hall
Blacksburg, Va. 24061-0205
(703) 231-5324

Central United States Earthquake
Consortium
P.O. Box 367
Marion, Ill. 62959
(618) 997-5659

Earthquake Engineering Research Institute
6431 Fairmount Avenue, Suite 7
El Cerrito, Calif. 94530-3624
(415) 525-3668

Getty Conservation Institute
4503 Glencoe Avenue
Marina del Rey, Calif. 90292
(213) 822-2299

Intermuseum Conservation Association
Allen Art Building
Oberlin, Ohio 44074
(216) 775-7331

National Center for Earthquake
Engineering Research
SUNY-Buffalo
Red Jacket Quad
Buffalo, N.Y. 14261
(716) 636-3391

National Conference of State Historic
Preservation Officers
444 North Capitol Street, N.W., Suite 332
Washington, D.C. 20001
(202) 624-5465

National Coordinating Council on
Emergency Management
7297 Lee Highway, Unit N
Falls Church, Va. 22042
(703) 533-7672

National Fire Protection Association
1 Batterymarch Park
Quincy, Mass. 02269
(617) 770-3000

Natural Hazards Research and
Applications Information Center
Institute of Behavioral Sciences, No. 6
Campus Box 482
University of Colorado
Boulder, Colo. 80309-0482
(303) 492-6818

National Institute for the Conservation of
Cultural Property
Collections Care Information Service
3299 K Street, N.W., Suite 403
Washington, D.C. 20007
(800) 421-1381, (202) 625-1495

National Preservation Institute
National Building Museum
Judiciary Square, N.W.
Washington, D.C. 20001
(202) 393-0038

National Trust for Historic Preservation
1785 Massachusetts Avenue, N.W.
Washington, D.C. 20036
(202) 673-4000

Mid-Atlantic Regional Office
6401 Germantown Avenue
Philadelphia, Pa. 19144
(215) 438-2886

Midwest Regional Office
53 West Jackson Boulevard, Suite 1135
Chicago, Ill. 60604
(312) 939-5547

Mountains/Plains Regional Office
511 16th Street, Suite 700
Denver, Colo. 80202
(303) 623-1504

> Texas/New Mexico Field Office
> 500 Main Street, Suite 606
> Fort Worth, Tex. 76102
> (817) 332-4398

Northeast Regional Office
45 School Street, 4th Floor
Boston, Mass. 02108
(617) 523-0885

Southern Regional Office
456 King Street
Charleston, S.C. 29403
(803) 722-8552

Western Regional Office
One Sutter Street, Suite 707
San Francisco, Calif. 94104
(415) 956-0610

Preservation Action
1350 Connecticut Avenue, N.W., Suite 401
Washington, D.C. 20036
(202) 659-0915

Society for the Preservation of New
England Antiquities
141 Cambridge Street
Boston, Mass. 02114
(617) 227-2956

Society of Architectural Historians
1232 Pine Street
Philadelphia, Pa. 19107-5944
(215) 735-0246

International Organizations

International Centre for the Study of
the Preservation and the Restoration of
Cultural Property (ICCROM)
13 Via di San Michele
00153 Rome, Italy

> U.S. Committee
> c/o Advisory Council on Historic
> Preservation
> 1100 Pennsylvania Avenue, N.W.
> Suite 803
> Washington, D.C. 20506
> (202) 786-0503

International Council of Museums (ICOM)
Ad Hoc Committee for Disaster Reduction
1, rue Miollis
75732 Paris, Cedex 15, France

> U.S. National Committee
> 1225 I Street, N.W., Suite 200
> Washington, D.C. 20005
> (202) 289-1818

International Council on Monuments and
Sites (ICOMOS)
75, rue du Temple
75003 Paris, France

> U.S. National Committee
> 1600 H Street, N.W.
> Washington, D.C. 20006
> (202) 842-1866

UNESCO
Cultural Heritage Division
1, place de Fontenoy
75700 Paris, France

United Nations Disaster Relief Office
Room S2935
New York, N.Y. 10017
(212) 963-5704

World Monuments Fund
174 East 80th Street
New York, N.Y. 10021
(212) 517-9367

Regional Conservation Centers

AMIGOS Bibliographic Council (Southwest)
11300 North Central Expressway, Suite 321
Dallas, Tex. 75243
(214) 750-6130

Conservation Center for Art and Historic
Artifacts (Mid-Atlantic)
264 South 23rd Street
Philadelphia, Pa. 19103
(215) 545-0613

Northeast Document Conservation Center
100 Brickstone Square
Andover, Mass. 01810-1428
(508) 470-1010

Pittsburgh Regional Library Center
(Western Pennsylvania, West Virginia,
Western Maryland)
103 Yost Boulevard
Pittsburgh, Pa. 15221
(412) 825-0600

Southeastern Library Network
400 Colony Square, Plaza Level
Atlanta, Ga. 30361-6301
(404) 892-0943

State Historic Preservation Offices

Alabama Historical Commission
725 Monroe Street
Montgomery, Ala. 36130-5101
(205) 261-3184

Alaska Department of Natural Resources
Division of Parks
Office of History and Archeology
P.O. Box 107001
Anchorage, Alaska 99510-7001
(907) 762-2622

American Samoa Department of Parks and
Recreation
P.O. Box 1268
Pago Pago, American Samoa 96799
(011) 684-633-1191

Arizona State Parks
800 West Washington, Suite 415
Phoenix, Ariz. 85007
(602) 542-4009

Arkansas Historic Preservation Program
The Heritage Center
225 East Markham Street, Suite 200
Little Rock, Ark. 72201
(701) 371-2763

California Department of Parks and
Recreation
Office of Historic Preservation
P.O. Box 942896
Sacramento, Calif. 94296-0001
(916) 445-8006

Colorado Historical Society
1300 Broadway
Denver, Colo. 80203
(303) 866-2136

Connecticut Historical Commission
59 South Prospect Street
Hartford, Conn. 06106
(203) 566-3005

Delaware Division of Historical
and Cultural Affairs
Hall of Records
Dover, Del. 19901
(302) 736-5313

District of Columbia Department of
Consumer and Regulatory Affairs
614 H Street, N.W., Suite 305
Washington, D.C. 20001
(202) 727-7360

Federated States of Micronesia
Palikir, Pohnpei, FM 96941
(011) 691-320-2343

Florida Division of Historical Resources
Department of State
R. A. Gray Building
500 South Bronaugh Street
Tallahassee, Fla. 32399-0250
(904) 488-1480

Georgia Department of Natural Resources
205 Butler Street, S.E.
Floyd Towers East, Suite 1252
Atlanta, Ga. 30334
(404) 656-3500

Guam Department of Parks and Recreation
490 Naval Hospital Road
Agana Heights, Guam 96910
(011) 671-477-9620

Hawaii Department of Land and Natural
Resources
P.O. Box 621
Honolulu, Hawaii 96809
(808) 548-6550

Idaho Historical Society
210 Main Street
Boise, Idaho 83702
(208) 334-3890

Illinois Historic Preservation Agency
Old State Capitol
Springfield, Ill. 62701
(217) 782-4836

Indiana Department of Natural Resources
608 State Office Building
Indianapolis, Ind. 46204
(317) 232-4020

Iowa State Historical Society
Capitol Complex
East Sixth and Locust Streets
Des Moines, Iowa 50319
(515) 281-5113

Kansas State Historical Society
120 West 10th Street
Topeka, Kans. 66612
(913) 296-3251

Kentucky Heritage Council
Capital Plaza Tower, 12th Floor
Frankfort, Ky. 40601-1967
(502) 564-7005

Louisiana Division of Culture
Recreation and Tourism
P.O. Box 44247
Baton Rouge, La. 70804
(504) 342-8200

Maine Historic Preservation Commission
55 Capitol Street, Station 65
Augusta, Maine 04333
(207) 289-2132

Marshall Islands
Alele Museum
Box 629
Majuro, Marshall Islands 96960
(011) 692-3326

Maryland Historical Trust
45 Calvert Street
Annapolis, Md. 21401
(301) 974-3644

Massachusetts Historical Commission
80 Boylston Street
Boston, Mass. 02116
(617) 727-8470

Michigan Bureau of History
Department of State
717 West Allegan
Lansing, Mich. 48918
(517) 373-6362

Minnesota Historical Society
690 Cedar Street
St. Paul, Minn. 55101
(612) 296-2747

Mississippi Department of Archives and
History
P.O. Box 571
Jackson, Miss. 39205
(601) 359-1424

Missouri State Department of Natural
Resources
1915 Southridge Drive
P.O. Box 176
Jefferson City, Mo. 65102
(314) 751-4422

Montana Historical Society
225 North Roberts
Helena, Mont. 59620-9990
(406) 444-7715

Nebraska State Historical Society
1500 R Street
P.O. Box 82554
Lincoln, Neb. 68501
(402) 471-4787

Nevada Department of Conservation and
Natural Resources
Nye Building, Room 213
201 South Fall Street
Carson City, Nev. 89710
(702) 885-4360

New Hampshire Division of Historical
Resources and State Historic Preservation
Walker Building
State Office Park South
15 South Fruit Street
P.O. Box 2043
Concord, N.H. 03301
(603) 271-3483

New Jersey Department of Environmental
Protection
401 East State Street, CN-402
Trenton, N.J. 08625
(609) 292-2885

New Mexico Office of Cultural Affairs
Historic Preservation Division
Villa Rivera
228 East Palace Avenue, Room 101
Santa Fe, N.M. 87503
(505) 827-8320

New York Office of Parks
Recreation and Historic Preservation
Agency
Empire State Plaza, Building 1
Albany, N.Y. 12238
(518) 474-0443

North Carolina Division of Archives and
History
Department of Cultural Resources
109 East Jones Street
Raleigh, N.C. 27611
(919) 733-7305

North Dakota State Historical Society
North Dakota Heritage Center
Bismarck, N.D. 58505
(701) 224-2667

Northern Mariana Islands Department of
Community and Cultural Affairs
Saipan, Mariana Islands 96950
(011) 670-322-9722

Ohio Historical Society
Historic Preservation Division
1985 Velma Avenue
Columbus, Ohio 43211
(614) 297-2470

Oklahoma Historical Society
Wiley Post Historical Building
2100 North Lincoln Boulevard
Oklahoma City, Okla. 73105
(405) 521-2491

Oregon State Parks and Recreation
525 Trade Street, S.E.
Salem, Ore. 97310
(503) 378-5019

Palau Bureau of Community Services
Ministry of Social Services
P.O. Box 100
Koror, Palau 96940
(011) 691-9489

Pennsylvania Historical and Museum
Commission
P.O. Box 1026
Harrisburg, Pa. 17108
(717) 787-2891

Puerto Rico Office of Historic Preservation
Box 82
La Fortaleza
San Juan, P.R. 00918
(809) 721-2676

Rhode Island Historical Preservation
Commission
Old State House
150 Benefit Street
Providence, R.I. 02903
(401) 277-2678

South Carolina Department of Archives
and History
1430 Senate Street
P.O. Box 11669
Columbia, S.C. 29211
(803) 734-8592

South Dakota State Historical Society
900 Governors Drive
Pierre, S.D. 57501
(605) 773-3458

Tennessee Department of Conservation
701 Broadway
Nashville, Tenn. 37219-5237
(615) 742-6758

Texas Historical Commission
Capitol Station
P.O. Box 12276
Austin, Tex. 78711
(512) 463-6100

Utah State Historical Society
300 Rio Grande
Salt Lake City, Utah 84101-1182
(801) 533-5755

Vermont Division for Historic Preservation
Pavilion Building
58 East State Street
Montpelier, Vt. 05602
(802) 828-3226

Virgin Islands Department of Planning and
Natural Resources
Division of Archeology and Historic
Preservation
179 Altona and Welgunst
St. Thomas, V.I. 00801
(809) 773-1082

Virginia Department of Historic Resources
221 Governor Street
Richmond, Va. 23219
(804) 786-3143

Washington Office of Archeology and
Historic Preservation
111 West 21st Avenue, KL-11
Olympia, Wash. 98504
(206) 753-4011

West Virginia Department of Culture and
History
Capitol Complex
Charleston, W.Va. 23305
(304) 348-0220

Wisconsin State Historical Society
816 State Street
Madison, Wis. 53706
(608) 262-1339

Wyoming Department of Archives
Museums and History
Barrett Building
2301 Central Avenue
Cheyenne, Wyo. 82002
(307) 777-7013

Statewide Preservation Organizations

Alabama Preservation Alliance
P.O. Box 2228
Montgomery, Ala. 36102
(205) 279-9881

Alaska Association for Historic Preservation
1326 K Street
Anchorage, Alaska 99501
(907) 257-2697

Arizona Preservation Foundation
P.O. Box 13492
Prescott, Ariz. 85002
(602) 253-5381

Historic Preservation Alliance of Arkansas
P.O. Box 305
Little Rock, Ark. 72203
(501) 372-4757

California Preservation Foundation
1615 Broadway, Suite 705
Oakland, Calif. 94612
(415) 763-0972

Colorado Preservation
P.O. Box 843
Denver, Colo. 80201-0843
(303) 757-9786

Connecticut Trust for Historic Preservation
152 Temple Street
New Haven, Conn. 06510
(203) 562-6312

Historical Society of Delaware
505 Market Street Mall
Wilmington, Del. 19801
(302) 655-7161

D.C. Preservation League
918 F Street, N.W., Suite 310
Washington, D.C. 20004
(202) 737-1519

Florida Trust for Historic Preservation
P.O. Box 11206
Tallahassee, Fla. 32302
(904) 224-8128

Georgia Trust for Historic Preservation
1516 Peachtree Street, N.W.
Atlanta, Ga. 30309
(404) 881-9980

Historic Hawaii Foundation
P.O. Box 1658
Honolulu, Hawaii 96806
(808) 537-9564

Idaho Historic Preservation Council
P.O. Box 1495
Boise, Idaho 83701
(208) 345-4698

Landmarks Preservation Council of Illinois
53 West Jackson Boulevard, Suite 752
Chicago, Ill. 60604
(312) 922-1742

Historic Landmarks Foundation of Indiana
3402 Boulevard Place
Indianapolis, Ind. 46208
(317) 926-2301

Kansas Preservation Alliance
P.O. Box 1000
Lawrence, Kans. 66044
(316) 343-1200

Commonwealth Preservation Advocates of
Kentucky
200 East Main Street
Lexington, Ky. 40507
(606) 258-3265

Louisiana Preservation Alliance
P.O. Box 1587
Baton Rouge, La. 70821
(504) 383-4476

Maine Citizens for Historic Preservation
P.O. Box 1198
Portland, Maine 04104
(207) 775-3652

Preservation Maryland
24 West Saratoga Street
Baltimore, Md. 21201
(301) 685-2886

Architectural Conservation Trust for
Massachusetts
45 School Street
Boston, Mass. 02108
(617) 523-8678

Historic Massachusetts
45 School Street
Boston, Mass. 02108
(617) 723-3383

Michigan Historic Preservation Network
P.O. Box 398
Clarkston, Mich. 48016
(313) 625-8181

Preservation Alliance of Minnesota
P.O. Box 10485
Minneapolis, Minn. 55458
(612) 931-9879

Missouri Alliance for Historic Preservation
P.O. Box 895
Jefferson City, Mo. 65102
(314) 635-687

Montana Preservation Alliance
Butte–Silver Bow Courthouse
P.O. Box 291
Butte, Mont. 59703
(406) 723-4061, ext. 313

Nebraska Preservation Council
11711 Arbor
Omaha, Neb. 68144
(402) 330-6330

Nevada Heritage
P.O. Box 352
Carson City, Nev. 89702
(702) 882-7895

Inherit New Hampshire
118 North Main Street
P.O. Box 268
Concord, N.H. 03301
(603) 224-2281

Preservation New Jersey
180 Township Line Road
Belle Mead, N.J. 08502
(201) 359-4557

New Mexico Preservation Coalition
P.O. Box 2748
Corrales, N.M. 87048

Preservation League of New York State
307 Hamilton Street
Albany, N.Y. 12210
(518) 462-5658

Landmark Society of Western New York
130 Spring Street
Rochester, N.Y. 14608
(716) 274-7764

Historic Preservation Foundation of North
Carolina
1804 Hillsborough Street
P.O. Box 27644
Raleigh, N.C. 27611-7644
(919) 832-3652

Ohio Preservation Alliance
297 South High Street
Columbus, Ohio 43215
(614) 221-0227

Historic Preservation League of Oregon
P.O. Box 40053
Portland, Ore. 97240
(503) 243-1923

Preservation Fund of Pennsylvania
2470 Kissell Hill Road
Lancaster, Pa. 17601
(717) 569-2243

Heritage Trust of Rhode Island
199 Hope Street
Providence, R.I. 02906
(401) 253-2707

Confederation of South Carolina Local
Historical Societies
P.O. Box 11669
Columbia, S.C. 29211
(803) 734-8577

Historic South Dakota Foundation
P.O. Box 2998
Rapid City, S.D. 57709
(605) 341-5820

Association for the Preservation of
Tennessee Antiquities
Belle Meade Mansion
110 Leake Avenue
Nashville, Tenn. 37205
(615) 352-8247

Tennessee Heritage Alliance
c/o Thomason and Associates
P.O. Box 121225
Nashville, Tenn. 37212

Preservation Texas Alliance
P.O. Box 12832
Austin, Tex. 78711
(713) 739-4615

Texas Historical Foundation
Center for Historic Resources
Texas A&M University
College of Architecture
College Station, Tex. 77843-3137
(409) 845-6025

Utah Heritage Foundation
355 Quince Street
Salt Lake City, Utah 84103
(801) 533-0858

Preservation Trust of Vermont
104 Church Street
Burlington, Vt. 05401
(802) 658-6647

St. Croix Landmarks Society
P.O. Box 2855
Frederiksted, St. Croix, V.I. 00840
(809) 772-0598

St. Thomas Historical Trust
P.O. Box 11849
Charlotte Amalie
St. Thomas, V.I. 00801
(809) 774-9139

Association for the Preservation of
Virginia Antiquities
2300 East Grace Street
Richmond, Va. 23223
(804) 648-1889

Preservation Alliance of Virginia
P.O. Box 295
Charlottesville, Va. 22902
(804) 979-3899

Washington Trust for Historic Preservation
204 First Avenue, South
Seattle, Wash. 98104
(206) 624-7880

Preservation Alliance of West Virginia
1500 Chapline Street
Wheeling, W.Va. 26003
(304) 234-3701

Wisconsin Trust for Historic Preservation
P.O. Box 32002
Franklin, Wis. 53132
(414) 425-3295

Further Reading

Advisory Council on Historic Preservation. *Disaster Management Program: Protecting Historic Resources at Risk*. Washington, D.C.: Advisory Council on Historic Preservation, 1990.

——————. *Fire Safety Retrofitting in Historic Buildings*. Washington, D.C.: Advisory Council on Historic Preservation and U.S. General Services Administration, 1989.

Architectural Resources Group. *An Assessment of Damage Caused to Historic Resources by the Loma Prieta Earthquake*. Washington, D.C.: National Trust for Historic Preservation, 1990.

Association of Art Museum Directors. *Planning for Emergencies: A Guide for Museums*. Richmond, Va.: Association of Art Museum Directors, 1987. Available from the American Association of Museums.

Barton, John P., and Johanna G. Wellheiser, eds. *An Ounce of Prevention: A Handbook on Disaster Contingency Planning for Archives, Libraries and Record Centres*. Toronto: Toronto Area Archivists Group Education Foundation (P.O. Box 97, Station F, Toronto, Ontario M4Y 2L4, Canada), 1985.

Bay Area Regional Earthquake Preparedness Project. "Local Building Officials' Guide to the Utilization of Volunteer Engineers." Oakland, Calif.: Bay Area Regional Earthquake Preparedness Project, 1989.

——————. "Reducing Hazards in Unreinforced Masonry Buildings" and "Reducing Hazards in Wood Frame Buildings." Hazardous Buildings Case Study Series. Oakland, Calif.: Bay Area Regional Earthquake Preparedness Project.

Bierce, C. Richard, AIA. *In Search of Huracán Hugo: An Assessment of Hurricane Damages to Historic Resources in the Commonwealth of Puerto Rico*. Washington, D.C.: National Trust for Historic Preservation, 1989.

Chapman, William. *The Impact of Hurricane Hugo on the Historic Resources of South Carolina and North Carolina*. Washington, D.C.: National Trust for Historic Preservation, 1989.

——————. "The Repair and Preservation of Vernacular Wood Buildings: With Special Attention to Buildings in Storm-prone Areas of the Southeastern U.S. and Caribbean." Washington, D.C.: National Trust for Historic Preservation, 1990.

Cohen, David, Doug Menuez and Ron Grant Tussy. *Fifteen Seconds: The Great California Earthquake of 1989*. Washington, D.C.: Island Press, 1989.

de Torres, Amparo R., ed. *Collections Care: A Selected Bibliography*. Washington, D.C.: National Institute for the Conservation of Cultural Property, 1990.

Federal Emergency Management Agency. *A Guide to Federal Aid in Disasters.* DAP 19. Washington, D.C.: FEMA, June 1990.

——————. *The CEO's Disaster Survival Kit.* Washington, D.C.: FEMA, 1988.

Feilden, Bernard M. *Between Two Earthquakes: Cultural Property in Seismic Zones.* Marina del Ray, Calif.: Getty Conservation Institute and ICCROM, 1987.

Flitner, Arthur. "An Insurance Primer for the Local Historical Organization," *History News,* January–February 1988. American Association for State and Local History.

Gjessing, Frederik C., and George F. Tyson. *Report on Hurricane Hugo's Impact on Historic Resources in the United States Virgin Islands, with Recommendations for Preservation Action.* Washington, D.C.: National Trust for Historic Preservation, 1989.

Godschalk, David R., David J. Brower and Timothy Beatley. *Catastrophic Coastal Storms: Hazard Mitigation and Development Management.* Chapel Hill, N.C.: Duke University Press, 1989.

Hanson, Gladys, and Emmet Condon. *Denial of Disaster.* San Francisco: Cameron and Company, 1989.

Hunter, John E. *Emergency Preparedness for Museums, Historic Sites and Archives: An Annotated Bibliography.* Nashville, Tenn.: American Association for State and Local History, 1979.

——————. "Museum Collections: Emergency Planning." In *National Park Service Museum Handbook,* Part I. Washington, D.C.: National Park Service, U.S. Department of the Interior, 1990.

J. Paul Getty Museum. *Emergency Planning Handbook.* Malibu, Calif.: J. Paul Getty Museum (P.O. Box 2112, Santa Monica, Calif. 90406), 1988.

Jones, Barclay G., ed. *Protecting Historic Architecture and Museum Collections from Natural Disasters.* Boston: Butterworth Publishers (80 Montvale Avenue, Stoneham, Mass. 02180), 1986.

Maddex, Diane, ed. *All About Old Buildings: The Whole Preservation Catalog.* Washington, D.C.: Preservation Press, 1985.

——————. *Landmark Yellow Pages: Where to Find All the Names, Addresses, Facts and Figures You Need.* Washington, D.C.: Preservation Press, 1990.

Martin, John H., and Charlene K. Edwards, eds. *The Corning Flood: Museum Under Water.* Corning, N.Y.: Corning Museum of Glass, 1979.

Merritt, John F. *History at Risk. Loma Prieta: Seismic Safety and Historic Buildings.* Oakland: California Preservation Foundation, 1990.

Mystic Seaport. *Hurricane and Storm Emergency Station Bill.* Mystic, Conn.: Mystic Seaport (Route 27, Mystic, Conn. 06355), 1989.

National Fire Protection Association. "Recommended Practice for the Protection of Libraries and Library Collections," "Recommended Practice for the Protection of Museums and Museum Collections," "Recommended Practice for the Protection of Historic Structures and Sites" and "Recommended Practice for Fire Protection in Rehabilitation and Adaptive Reuse of Historic Structures." Boston: National Fire Protection Association.

National Institute for the Conservation of Cultural Property. *Directory of Members, 1991.* Washington, D.C.: National Institute for the Conservation of Cultural Property, 1990.

—————. *Disaster Preparedness Bibliography.* Washington, D.C.: National Institute for the Conservation of Cultural Property, 1990.

National Register of Historic Places. "Guidelines for Local Surveys: A Basis for Preservation Planning." National Register Bulletin 24. Washington, D.C.: National Park Service, U.S. Department of the Interior, 1977.

National Trust for Historic Preservation. *The Impact of Hurricane Hugo on Historic Places: An Assessment of Damages in North Carolina, South Carolina, Puerto Rico and the United States Virgin Islands.* Washington, D.C.: National Trust for Historic Preservation, 1990.

Preservation Assistance Division. *Maintaining Historic Buildings: An Annotated Bibliography.* Compiled by Kaye Ellen Simonson. Washington, D.C.: National Park Service, U.S. Department of the Interior, 1990.

—————. *The Secretary of the Interior's Standards for Rehabilitation and Guidelines for Rehabilitating Historic Buildings.* 1976. Rev. ed. Washington, D.C.: National Park Service, U.S. Department of the Interior, 1990.

U.S. Geological Survey. *The Next Big Earthquake in the Bay Area May Come Sooner Than You Think: Are You Prepared?* Newspaper supplement published in cooperation with the American Red Cross and United Way. Menlo Park, Calif.: USGS (Earthquakes, 345 Middlefield Road, Menlo Park, Calif. 94025), 1990. Available in English, Spanish, Chinese, Braille and Recordings for the Blind.

Young, Richard F. *Library and Archival Disaster-Preparedness and Recovery.* Videotape and workbook set. Oakton, Va.: BiblioPrep Films (11420 Vale Road, Suite D, Oakton, Va. 22124), 1986.

Sources

In addition to resources mentioned in the text, the following provided helpful information in the preparation of this book. Complete citations for shortened references appear in Further Reading.

CHAPTER 1

Key sources: Architectural Resources Group. *An Assessment of Damage Caused to Historic Resources by the Loma Prieta Earthquake*; C. Richard Bierce, AIA. *In Search of Huracán Hugo*; William Chapman. *The Impact of Hurricane Hugo on the Historic Resources of South Carolina and North Carolina*; Frederik C. Gjessing and George F. Tyson. *Report on Hurricane Hugo's Impact on Historic Resources in the United States Virgin Islands*; National Trust. *The Impact of Hurricane Hugo on Historic Places.*

Other sources: Barclay G. Jones, ed. *Protecting Historic Architecture and Museum Collections from Natural Disasters*; J. Jackson Walter. "Keeping America's Heritage Alive." Speech, Ford Hall Forum, Boston, November 9, 1989.

Periodical articles: Michael Adlerstein. "Bi-coastal Disaster Assistance," *Cultural Resources Management Bulletin*, No. 1, 1990. National Park Service; Arnold Berke. "Nature's Wrecking Ball," *Preservation News*, November 1989. National Trust; California Preservation Foundation. "After Loma Prieta — A Special Quake Issue." Newsletter supplement, January 1990; Nora Richter Greer. "Recent Natural Disasters Give Insight to Preservationists," *Forum Newsletter*, December 1989. National Trust; Thomas W. Sweeney. "Charleston on the Mend," *Historic Preservation*, September–October, 1990. National Trust; Thomas W. Sweeney. "Nature's Wrecking Ball (Cont.)," *Preservation News*, December 1989. National Trust.

CHAPTER 2

Key sources: Barclay G. Jones, ed. *Protecting Historic Architecture and Museum Collections from Natural Disasters*; Frank W. Lane. *The Violent Earth*. Topsfield, Mass.: Salem House Publishers, 1986; Tony Waltham. *Catastrophe: The Violent Earth*. New York: Crown Publishers, 1978.

Other sources: Bay Area Regional Earthquake Preparedness Project. "Reducing Hazards in Unreinforced Masonry Buildings," n.d.; *Information Please Almanac*. Boston: Houghton Mifflin, 1990; National Trust. *The Impact of Hurricane Hugo on Historic Places.*

Periodical article: Barclay G. Jones. "Litany of Losses," *Museum News*, May–June 1990. American Association of Museums.

CHAPTER 3

Key sources: *Ashton Villa (Galveston, Tex.) Disaster Preparedness Plan.* June 1990; John A. Blume. "The Mitigation and Prevention of Earthquake Damage to Artifacts." In Jones, 1986; L. Neal FitzSimons, FASCE. "Multi-hazard Assessment of Localities and Sites." In Jones, 1986; Melvyn Green, P.E. "Reducing Vulnerability." In Jones, 1986. John E. Hunter. "Museum Collections: Emergency Planning." In *National Park Service Museum Handbook,* Part I; Barclay G. Jones. "Assessing Dangers" and "Preventing Damage." In Jones, 1986; Barclay G. Jones, ed. *Protecting Historic Architecture and Museum Collections from Natural Disasters.*

Other sources: American Society of Home Inspectors. "Maintaining Your Home: Some Suggestions." Washington, D.C.: Author, n.d.; Bay Area Regional Earthquake Preparedness Project. "Reducing Hazards in Unreinforced Masonry Buildings"; Ben Boozer. "Planning for Natural Disasters." Washington, D.C.: National Trust, 1990; Jan Coggeshall, former mayor, Galveston, Tex. Interview, September 1990; Wilbur Faulk. "How the J. Paul Getty Museum Plans and Prepares for Major Emergencies." Unpublished abstract prepared for American Association of Museums annual meeting, Chicago, June 1990; J. Paul Getty Museum. *Emergency Planning Handbook;* Frank W. Lane. *The Violent Earth.* Topsfield, Mass.: Salem House Publishers, 1986; John F. Merritt. *History at Risk;* Patricia L. Miller. "Emergency Preparedness in Museums and Historic Sites." *Technical Insert,* November–December 1989. Illinois Heritage Association; Toby Murray. "Disaster Preparedness: A Checklist." Oklahoma Field Advisory Service Technical Bulletin 2. Oklahoma Museums Association and Oklahoma Historical Society, n.d.; Richard F. Young. *Library and Archival Disaster-Preparedness and Recovery.*

Periodical articles: William Chapman. "How Many Historic Buildings Are There?," *Preservation Forum,* Fall 1990. National Trust; Nora Richter Greer. "Recent Natural Disasters Give Insight to Preservationists," *Forum Newsletter,* December 1989. National Trust; "Hurricane and Earthquake Victims Can Deduct Passive Losses," *Client's Monthly Alert,* August 1990; "Insuring Gardens," *Garden Design,* Spring 1990; Forrest M. Mims III. "The Amateur Scientist: A Remote-Control Camera that Catches the Wind and Captures the Landscape," *Scientific American,* October 1990; Cris Oppenheimer-Pitthan. "Know Where You Stand With Earthquake Insurance," *San Jose Mercury News,* October 24, 1989; U.S. Geological Survey. *The Next Big Earthquake in the Bay Area May Come Sooner Than You Think: Are You Prepared?*

CHAPTER 4

Key sources: Barclay G. Jones, ed. *Protecting Historic Architecture and Museum Collections from Natural Disasters;* Mystic Seaport. *Hurricane and Storm Emergency Station Bill.*

Other sources: Perry E. Borchers. "Applying Photogrammetry to the Protection of Historic Architecture and Museum Collections from Earthquakes and Other Natural Disasters." In Jones, 1986; Kathryn A. Burns. Testimony before the Santa Cruz, Calif., City Council, November 2, 1989; "FEMA Disaster Assistance and the Protection of Historic Properties." State of California Office of Historic Preservation, Department of Parks and Recreation, 1989; Federal Emergency Management Agency. *A Guide to Federal Aid in Disasters;* Barclay G. Jones. "Seeking Assistance" and "Confronting Emergencies." In Jones, 1986; Richard W. Krimm. "Federal Response Measures to Natural Disasters." In Jones, 1986; John W. Meffert. Preservation Society of Charleston. Interview, August 1990.

Periodical articles: "Be Careful with Old Architecture," *San Francisco Examiner*, Editorial, October 30, 1989; Foundation for San Francisco's Architectural Heritage. "Earthquake '89," *Heritage Newsletter*, Vol. XVII, No. 4; Barclay G. Jones. "Litany of Losses," *Museum News*, May–June 1990; Chuck Smith-Kim. "The Hidden Damage: What to Look for Even if Your House Appears Unscathed," *San Francisco Examiner*, Real Estate, October 22, 1989; Thomas A. Vitanza. "NPS Surveys Yield Data on the Effects of Hurricane Hugo," *Courier*, 1990, No. 1. National Park Service; John C. Williams. "Charleston Looks to Spring Recovery," *New York Times*, Travel, October 8, 1989.

CHAPTER 5

Key sources: National Trust. *The Impact of Hurricane Hugo on Historic Places*; U.S. Department of the Interior, National Park Service. "Emergency Stabilization and Conservation Measures." Prepared for the Historic Charleston Foundation, September 29, 1989.

Other sources: Charles Edwin Chase. Architecture and Preservation Division, Charleston, S.C. Interview, August 1990; Federal Emergency Management Agency. *A Guide to Federal Aid in Disasters*; J. Paul Getty Museum. *Emergency Planning Handbook*; National Institute for the Conservation of Cultural Property. Annual meeting, Washington, D.C., October 17, 1990; Helaine Kaplan Prentice and Blair Prentice. *Rehab Right: How to Realize the Full Value of Your Old House.* 1978. Rev. ed. Berkeley, Calif.: Ten Speed Press, 1986; Preservation Assistance Division, National Park Service. *The Secretary of the Interior's Standards for Rehabilitation and Guidelines for Rehabilitating Historic Buildings*; David Prowler. "A Brief Description of the Unreinforced Masonry Building Safety Project," Nels Roselund. "Strengthening Unreinforced Brick Bearing Wall Buildings to Resist Earthquake Forces," and Kenneth Topping. "Preservation Issues and Earthquake Recovery and Reconstruction Planning." Papers delivered at Living on the Faultline Conferences, 1990; San Francisco Landmarks Preservation Advisory Board. Postearthquake advisory materials, 1989–90; Natalie Shivers. *Walls and Molding: How to Care for Old and Historic Wood and Plaster.* Washington, D.C.: Preservation Press, 1990.

Periodical articles: "A Few Trees Saved, Many More Lost," *San Juan Star*, October 2, 1989; Arnold Berke. "History on the Mend: Hugo, Quake Victims Work to Save and Rebuild." *Preservation News*, May 1990. National Trust; California Preservation Foundation. "Earthquake Shakes Sacramento." *California Preservation*, Vol. 15, No. 1, January 1990; Sarah Fick. "In the Midst of Recovery, Sullivan's Island Plans Its Future," *Preservation Forum*, Fall 1990. National Trust; Jane Gross. "San Francisco Limps in Repair of Damage Months After Quake," *New York Times*, August 15, 1990, and "A Year Later, Bay Area Jumps at Tiny Rattles," *New York Times*, October 14, 1990; Hannah Heywood. "Building Above Code Helped Save House," *Charleston (S.C.) Post-Courier*, October 29, 1989; Hannah Heywood and Chris Sosnowski. "Codes Basically Sound, But Fine Tuning Needed," *Charleston (S.C.) Post-Courier*, n.d.; Mark Mayfield. "Recovery from Storm Is Steady, Painful," *USA Today*, September 20, 1990; National Roofing Contractors Association. "DART Program Hits Target in Charleston Building Restoration," *Professional Roofing*, n.d.; Arlie Porter. "Harvest of Hugo-downed Trees Nears End," *Charleston (S.C.) Post-Courier*, July 30, 1990; "Resource Directory," *Preservation Forum*, Fall 1987; Elizabeth Roman. "Hurricane Damage to Landscaping Should Be Assessed and Taken Care of as Soon as Possible to Save Old Trees, Plant New Ones," *Caribbean Business*, October 5, 1989; Nancy L. Ross. "Rebuilding in Charleston After the Hurricane," *Washington Post*, Washington Home, June 14, 1990; "Slate Roofing Panel Seminar," *Preservation Progress*,

October 16, 1989. Preservation Society of Charleson; Chuck Smith-Kim. "Bracing for the Next One," *San Francisco Examiner*, Real Estate, October 29, 1989; Thomas W. Sweeney. "History on the Mend: Hugo, Quake Victims Work to Save and Rebuild," *Preservation News*, May 1990. National Trust; U.S. Geological Survey. *The Next Big Earthquake in the Bay Area May Come Sooner Than You Think: Are You Prepared?* ; Betsy Wade. "Charleston Comeback: It's Ready for Spring," *New York Times*, February 11, 1990; James T. Yenckel. "Fearless Traveler," *Washington Post*, April 1, 1990.

CHAPTER 6

Key sources: Advisory Council on Historic Preservation. *Disaster Management Program: Protecting Historic Resources at Risk;* John F. Merritt, *History at Risk.*

Other sources: Architectural Resources Group. *An Assessment of Damage Caused to Historic Resources by the Loma Prieta Earthquake;* C. Richard Bierce, AIA. *In Search of Huracán Hugo;* William Chapman. *The Impact of Hurricane Hugo on the Historic Resources of South Carolina and North Carolina;* Frederik C. Gjessing and George F. Tyson. *Report on Hurricane Hugo's Impact on Historic Resources in the United States Virgin Islands;* John E. Hunter. "Museum Collections: Emergency Planning." In *National Park Service Museum Handbook*, Part I; National Trust. *The Impact of Hurricane Hugo on Historic Places.*

Periodical article: Robert E. Litan. "Earthquake! Planning and Paying for the 'Big One,'" *The Brookings Review*, Fall 1990.

Index

Page numbers in italics refer to illustrations and captions.